Early Childhood Studies Reflective Reader

Edited by
MARY WILD
and
HELENA MITCHELL

LearningMatters

First published in 2007 by Learning Matters Ltd.
Reprinted in 2008

British Library Cataloguing in Publication Data
A CIP record for this book is available from the British Library.

ISBN: 978 1 84445 119 7

Cover and text design by Code 5 Design Associates Ltd
Project management by Deer Park Productions, Tavistock, Devon
Typeset by Pantek Arts Ltd, Maidstone, Kent
Printed and bound in Great Britain by Bell & Bain Ltd, Glasgow

Learning Matters Ltd
33 Southernhay East
Exeter EX1 1NX
Tel: 01392 215560
info@learningmatters.co.uk
www.learningmatters.co.uk

Contents

The Authors

Rachel Friedman is Senior Lecturer in Early Years at Oxford Brookes University, and has shared responsibility for equal opportunities and diversity across Westminster Institute of Education, one of the schools of the university. She contributes to the Early Childhood Studies Degree, the Foundation Degree in Early Years, the Early Years strand of the PGCE, and Early Years Professional Status provision. She has had a wide range of international Early Years experience, working in a variety of public and private programmes with children from birth through to age five. She is currently a doctoral student at the University of London's Institute of Education.

Helena Mitchell is Academic Group Head for Child Development and Education at Oxford Brookes University. Helena has been involved in the development of a range of courses focused on Early Years at Oxford Brookes University, and was responsible for establishing the Early Childhood Studies degree in 2000. She is a member of the Oxfordshire EYDCP, and chairs the county's Workforce Development Forum. She previously worked as an infant teacher and deputy headteacher of a large nursery and infants school. She has recently been involved in research projects on student employability with ESCalate, practitioners' views on appropriate training, and is a member of the British Educational Research Association (BERA). She is a member of the Early Childhood Studies Degrees Network, which brings together course leaders of the ECS degrees from across the UK.

Carolyn Silberfeld has extensive experience of roles within both health and education sectors. Since 2000 she has been Programme Leader of the BA Early Childhood Studies at University of East London. She is active within the local community as a member of Barking & Dagenham Early Years Partnership and three Sure Start evaluation projects. During the past ten years, Carolyn has co-ordinated a number of student exchanges to France and the Netherlands, and has been the project co-ordinator (Europe) for the EU: Canada Student Exchange Programme. Carolyn is Treasurer of the Early Childhood Studies Degrees Network.

Nick Swarbrick is Senior Lecturer in Early Years at Oxford Brookes University, and is the course leader for the Foundation Degree in Early Years. He has also had a lead role in developing the Early Years strand of the Primary PGCE Programme, and is Lead Assessor for the Early Years Professional Programme. Before taking up his present post at Oxford Brookes, he was headteacher of a small, multicultural and multilingual nursery school in Oxford City. His present research interests concern the history of Early Years education in the UK, and the use of outdoor space to promote children's learning and well-being.

Mary Wild is the Course Leader for the Early Childhood Studies degree course at Oxford Brookes University. She also contributes to the Foundation Degree in Early Years, the Early Years strand of the PGCE, Early Years Professional Status provision, and the Advanced Specialism in Early Years. Mary is a qualified teacher with experience in both the primary and Early Years sectors. Her DPhil at Oxford University investigated the use of ICT in Early Years classrooms. Additional research interests include early childhood literacy. Mary is also a member of the British Psychological Society and the British Educational Research Association (BERA). She is a member of the Early Childhood Studies Degrees Network, which brings together course leaders of the ECS degrees from across the UK.

Acknowledgements

Chapter 1

'Start Right: The Importance of Early Learning' in *Findings* (1994). Reprinted by kind permission of RSA, London: pp75–6

DfES, *Choice for parents, the best start for children: a 10yr strategy for child-care* (2004) Para 2.13–2.21. Reproduced under the terms of PSI Licence C2006007372

Ball, S. J. & Vincent, C. 'New Labour, Social Justice and the Childcare Market' (2005): reprinted by permission of the publisher (Taylor & Francis Ltd, http://www.informaworld.com) 31, 5 *British Educational Research Journal*: 558–560

Office of Children's Commissioner, *Annual report 2006* **www.childrenscommissioner.org**

Chapter 2

Every Child Matters: Children's Trusts **http://www.everychildmatters.gov.uk/aims/ childrenstrusts**. Reproduced under the terms of PSI Licence C2006007372

Anning, A. et al. Developing Multiprofessional Teamwork for Integrated Children's Services, Open University Press (2006). Reproduced with the kind permission of the Open University Press: pp115–117

A New Deal for Children? Cohen, B., et al. (2004). Reprinted by kind permission of The Policy Press, Bristol: pp8–9

Weinberger, J., Pickstone, C. and Hannon, P. (2005) *Learning from Sure Start*. Open University Press. Reproduced with the kind permission of the Open University Press Publishing Company: pp254ii–256

Chapter 3

Piaget, J. & Inhelder, B. *The Psychology of the Child*, 153 (1966). Routledge & Kegan Paul. Reproduced by permission of Taylor & Francis Books UK: pp5–6, 153

Donaldson, M., The Children's Minds (1987). Fontana. Reprinted by permission of HarperCollins Publishers Ltd: pp19–24, and Professor Martin Hughes for permission to quote from 'Egocentrism in pre-school children' (doctoral dissertation, 1975) with diagrams.

Vygotsky, L. S., *Mind in Society. The Development of Higher Psychological Processes*, edited by Michael Cole, Vera John-Steiner, Sylvia Scribner and Ellen Souberman, Cambridge, Mass.: Harvard University Press. Reprinted by permission from the publisher. Copyright © (1978) by the President and Fellows of Harvard College: pp85–86

Trevarthen, C. 'The Childrens Need to Learn a Culture' in Woodhead, M., Faulkner, D. & Littleton, K. (eds) (1998). *Cultural Worlds of Early Childhood*. Routledge & Kegan Paul. Reproduced by permission of Taylor & Francis Books UK: pp87–9

Chapter 4

British Medical Association, *Growing up in Britain: Ensuring a Healthy Future for our Children* (1999) Blackwell Publishing: pp17–19, 29–30

Hall, D & Ellman, D. (eds) 'Secondary Prevention: Early Detection and the Role of Screening' in *Health For All Children*, 4th edn, Oxford University Press (2006). Copyright © Royal College of Paediatrics and Child Health, 2003. Reprinted by kind permission of Oxford University Press: pp132–134

Panter-Brick, C. (ed), Biosocial Perspectives on Children. Copyright © Cambridge University Press 1998. Reprinted with permission: pp66–70

Chapter 5

Rutter, M. Copyright © (1972) *Maternal Deprivation Reassessed*. Reprinted by kind permission of Penguin Books UK: pp19–24

Bowlby, J. *Child Care and the Growth of Love*. Copyright © Bowlby (1953). Reprinted by kind permission of Penguin Books UK: pp26–28

Dunn, J., *Sisters & Brothers*. Copyright © 1985 by Judy Dunn. 1984. Reprinted by permission of HarperCollins Publishers Ltd: pp14–16

Bronfenbrenner, U., *The Ecology of Human Development. Experiments by Nature & Design*, Cambridge, Mass. Harvard University Press. Reprinted by permission from the publisher. Copyright © (1979) by the President and Fellows of Harvard College: pp3–4

Chapter 6

Clark, A. & Moss, P., *Listening to Young Children: The Mosaic Approach* (2001). Reprinted with permission from the National Children's Bureau: pp63–67

Paley, V. G., *A Child's Work: The Importance of Fantasy Play*. Copyright © (2004) by the University of Chicago. Reprinted by kind permission of the University of Chicago Press: pp16–19

Anning, A. & Ring, K., *Making Sense of Children's Drawing*. Open University Press 2004. Reproduced with the kind permission of the Open University Press Publishing Company: pp122–124

Elfer, P., Goldschmeid, E. & Selleck, D., *Key persons in the Nursery: Building relationships for quality provision*. Copyright © (2003) David Fulton. Reproduced by permission of Taylor & Francis Books UK: pp18–21, 23–29

Van Ausdale, D. and Feagin, J. R., (2001) 'How Adults View Children' in *The First R: How Children Learn Race & Racism*, reprinted by kind permission of Rowman & Littlefield: pp159–160

Chapter 7

Vygotsky, L. S. 'Play and its role in the mental development of the child' in *Play: Its Role in Development and Evolution*. Copyright © (1976) by Bruner, J., Jolly, A. and Sylva, K. (eds). New York: Penguin: p552, 19

Bruce, T., *Developing Learning in Early Childhood*, Copyright © Bruce (2004) Paul Chapman Publishing. Reproduced by permission of SAGE Publications, London, Los Angeles, New Delhi and Singapore: pp148–150

Nutbrown, C., *Threads of Thinking*. Copyright © Nutbrown (2006) Paul Chapman Publishing. Reproduced by permission of SAGE Publications, London, Los Angeles, New Delhi and Singapore: pp10–11

Kitson, N., 'Fantasy Play and the Case for Adult Intervention' in Moyles, J., *The Excellence of Play* 2nd edn. Open University Press (2005). Reproduced with the kind permission of the Open University Press Publishing Company: pp119–120

Chapter 8

DFES (2007), The early years Foundation Stage Practice Guidance 00012 (2007) BK7T-EN: pp6, 7. Reproduced under the terms of PSI Licence C2006007372

Waterland, L., *Not a Perfect Offering: A New School Year*. Thimble Press, (1994): pp77–8

Bilton, H., *Outdoor Play in the Early Years*. Copyright © (2002) David Fulton. Reproduced by permission of Taylor & Francis Books UK pp76–79

Brooker, L. 'Learning to be Child: Cultural Diversity & Early Years Ideology' in Yelland (ed) *Critical Issues in Early Childhood Education* Open University Press (2005). Reproduced with the kind permission of the Open University Press Publishing Company: p118

Introduction

Mary Wild

Knowledge ... is not just what we store inertly in our heads. It also provides a launching pad into the realm of the possible. (Bruner, 2007)

Putting together a collection of readings around the study of early childhood could easily be driven solely by the imperative of presenting a neat package of core readings and ideas for the subject. Any tutor of Early Childhood or Early Years Studies would recognise the desire amongst students for a collection of 'must read' texts. However, this is not the principal aim of thus reflective reader.

So what is the purpose of this reader? The purpose lies within the spirit of the opening quote from Bruner, that is, that it will serve as a launch pad for you, the reader; a starting point from which you will explore your own thoughts about the study, and indeed nature, of early childhood. The hope is that what you read will cause you to reflect on your own understanding of, and professional practice with, young children.

In the lecture by Bruner from which the quote is drawn he talks about the importance of 'making the strange familiar and the familiar strange' in broadening the bounds of our thinking. As you read through this reader you will find ideas which may at first seem strange or are unfamiliar but which as you read will be explored and explained in order to render them 'familiar'. You will also come across ideas that may seem wholly familiar to you as a practitioner or student within early years but you will be invited to think about these in different, 'unfamiliar' ways. Underlying this approach is the belief that to be a truly effective student or practitioner you need to be prepared both to seek out new ideas and to question existing ones.

Accompanying this philosophical remit, there is, of course, the practical recognition of the need to introduce students to some key readings within the field but there is also the realisation that a single definitive guide is not possible. The sheer breadth of the field of early childhood covering psychological and sociological perspectives, spanning education and care and embracing issues of policy and practice renders this an inherently impossible task. Equally, within each of these individually rich domains of knowledge the selection of readings can only be partial and indicative, and yet must simultaneously seek to make the important connections that exist between these seemingly disparate strands. We have set out therefore to introduce you to some key readings within four thematic areas that give a sense of the broad scope of the relatively new academic discipline that is Early Childhood Studies. Throughout the Reader you will find reference to other reading that you may wish to explore in order to deepen your understanding of the concepts and issues that are introduced.

As a discrete academic discipline Early Childhood Studies is still a relatively new area, though it draws on some academic traditions that are well established. This balance is reflected in the readings that are included in the different chapters within the four themes.

Some chapters will focus on classic long-established texts and invite you to reach your own conclusions about often disputed theory. Other chapters will encourage you to reflect on more recent developments particularly in relation to policy and practice within Early Years.

The first thematic area is **National initiatives**. Within this theme, Chapter 1 highlights the many different policy initiatives that have been focused on young children and their families over the course of the last decade. Anyone who has been working within Early Years over this period will be all too familiar with this policy spotlight and whilst welcoming the policy priority given to Early Years, may well have struggled at times to keep up with developments. This chapter will provide a welcome chance to pause, reflect and take stock of some of these initiatives, including the Ten Year Strategy for Childcare (DfES, 2004a). Chapter 2 focuses on one particular aspect of recent policy direction – the need for multi-professional working within Early Years that has been born in particular of the Every Child Matters Framework (DfES, 2004b). Here you will be encouraged to consider both the potential opportunities and the practical challenges of working in this way.

From the context of debate around current initiatives the second theme, **Development in the Early Years**, moves to the consideration of more perennial debates around the nature of learning. Firstly, in Chapter 3 you are introduced to some of the major theoretical accounts of learning. There is no shortage of summaries of such theories available but by reading extracts from the original theorists themselves you will be able to develop your own critical perspective towards what can seem to be abstract theory and debate and to make links between theory and practice. It is vital, however, that Early Childhood Studies does not become a discipline that is dominated by the discourse and culture of education and so in Chapter 4 the emphasis shifts to a focus on health. An important aspect of this chapter is the way in which you are asked to adopt a critically sceptical stance, thinking about the appropriateness, for example, of some of the definitions around health that can come to be accepted without challenge and may thereby dull our ability to evaluate both policy and practice.

A more sociological perspective emerges in the third theme, **Children and families**. The opening chapter in this theme, Chapter 5, looks at the family and its role in development. The idea of considering our underlying definitions suggested already in Chapter 4 is revisited here, as you are asked to reflect on what exactly we mean by the term 'the family'. The chapter presents extracts that enable you to see how influential theories, through the example of attachment theory, come to be challenged and developed. As the chapter develops you also have the chance to reflect on the importance of different relationships within the family and on the interaction between families and wider society. The second chapter in this theme signals a significant shift in emphasis. Having covered, in other chapters, issues of policy towards and around children and theoretical understandings of children, this chapter highlights the absolute imperative of actually listening to the children that we theorise about or make policy for. It sensitively invites you to explore your own practice in this respect and to pose questions about how we actually enable children to be not only heard but also genuinely listened to and empowered.

Building on the understandings of the centrality of the child established in Chapter 6, theme four of the book, **A curriculum for early learning**, sets out to consider the nature of the curriculum that is offered to our young children in the UK. In Chapter 7 the role of play in learning is explored. Some of the major theories around the role of play, including some of those theorists already covered in Chapter 3, are considered and you are invited to examine your own beliefs about the importance of children's play. The ways in which theories of play and learning have informed and influenced current and past practice in UK curriculum design are the focus of the second chapter within this theme, which considers formal and informal curricula and provides an opportunity for you to reflect on the types of learning experiences that we provide, or not, for our children.

A final, concluding chapter returns to the primary theme and purpose of the reader by inviting you to reflect on what it means to be a reflective professional in the Early Years. The notion of professionalism has resonance with the current initiative led by the government to establish the new Early Years Professional Status (EYPS), which is a status that is intended to be equivalent to Qualified Teacher Status (CWDC, 2006). Within the set of Professional Standards (CWDC, 2007) that has been drawn up to accompany this new status there is an emphasis on demonstrating knowledge and understanding about the principles that underpin effective practice and the ability to reflect on one's professional development. In this context it is hoped that this Reader will act as a support for practitioners who are working towards qualifying for EYPS. You will therefore find that each chapter has been linked to relevant EYPS standards from the six areas denoted within the Standards: Knowledge and understanding; Effective practice; Relationships with children; Communicating and working with families and carers; Teamwork and collaboration; and Professional development.

However, all of the contributing authors are convinced that being a professional is about more than simply meeting a set of external criteria. The capacity continually to ask oneself what it really means to be a professional within the Early Years, to continue enquiring about why you do things the way you do in your practice and to probe your beliefs and philosophy of childhood is of fundamental importance. Knowing that there are always 'other ways of knowing' (Bruner, 2007, ibid.) or indeed doing, rather than only one perspective that is 'true', or one prescriptive way of doing things that is valid, is the key message that we hope you will take from this Reader.

REFERENCES

Bruner, J. (2007) Cultivating the possible. Lecture presented at Dedication Ceremony for the Opening of the Jerome Bruner Building for the Department of Educational Studies, Oxford University. Oxford 13.03.07.

CWDC (2006) *A head start for all. Early Years Professional Status.* Candidate Information. Leeds: CWDC.

CWDC (2007) *Guidance to the standards for the award of Early Years Professional Status.* Leeds: CWDC.

DfES (2004a) *Choice for parents, the best start for children: A Ten Year Strategy for Childcare.* London: HMSO.

DfES (2004b) *Every Child Matters: Change For Children.* Nottingham: DfES Publications.

Chapter 1

The role of policymakers: rights and responsibilities

Helena Mitchell

In the past ten years there have been a huge number of initiatives focused on young children and their families. This chapter will consider the range of initiatives, reasons for them, and some of the outcomes that have resulted. It will also include consideration of the important role played by the United Nations Convention on the Rights of the Child (UNCRC) and the newly established Children's Commissioners.

OBJECTIVES

By the end of this chapter you should have:
- gained an overview of the policy drivers that have led to major changes in children's services;
- critically evaluated the impact of one of these initiatives on children and families;
- an overview of the different contexts which young children and families may encounter;
- reflected upon the role of Children's Commissioners and the impact of the United Nations Convention on the Rights of the Child.

Professional Standards for EYPS: S4, S5, S6, S18, S23

Make a list of all the different contexts you can think of in which young children may be educated and cared for outside the home. There is a range of very different possibilities, ranging from childminders who may care for a small number of children, to large day nurseries where there may be many children between the ages of three months and five years. Other contexts include nursery schools, Foundation Stage units, and children's centres which bring together a range of services for children and families.

Introduction

Over the past ten years, there have been vast and far-reaching changes to the provision of services for children and families. These changes have been largely driven by the Labour government, first elected in 1997, and focused upon eradicating poverty by increasing employment levels, particularly for mothers of young children. You may have come across some of the resulting initiatives, and may indeed have been involved in working with young children, for example, in an integrated setting. An integrated setting may include a day nursery, a nursery school, adult education classes, access to a health visitor, a drop-in family centre and crèche, antenatal classes, baby massage, an after-school club, amongst other services. The first integrated settings were the Early Excellence Centres in the late 1990s, based on nursery provision judged to be of the highest quality by OFSTED. Many were trailblazers for the notion of integration, but have been superseded by children's centres, which are part of a development programme across England.

Policy drivers

The National Childcare Strategy, introduced in 1998, was ultimately intended to improve educational outcomes for children. The government's intention here was that if parents were earning an income, rather than existing on benefits, quality of life would be improved for them and their children. This would lead to better health, welfare, and ultimately to better educational attainment for children (Cohen et al., 2004). Being in employment has a powerful impact on the ways in which parents view themselves, and the ways in which their children perceive their parents and their future life opportunities. Employment not only provides income, it can also bolster self-esteem and lead to increased social activity. Drawing on data from longitudinal studies conducted in the 1950s and 1960s (HM Treasury, 2004), which demonstrated that growing up in poverty or a low-income household increased the likelihood of low economic achievement in adulthood, gave strong support for increasing employment amongst parents in order to boost economic viability. Lone parents, especially lone mothers, were viewed as needing to be encouraged to seek employment or to return to the labour market in order to improve the economic circumstances for themselves and their children. Furthermore, there is also some evidence that poor economic circumstances impact upon cognitive development.

For these reasons, the newly elected Labour government began to put into place a number of measures to encourage unemployed parents into employment. Clearly, if parents with young children are to be employed they need to have access to childcare so that their children can be looked after while they are working. Furthermore, that childcare needs to be affordable and of good quality. But the pattern of childcare and education in the UK has a history of splintered and uneven provision. For many parents, returning to employment might not be a viable economic option because the cost of childcare would be greater than the salary they might achieve. And the quality and quantity of provision has been variable. Initiatives aimed at developing childcare and education for children younger than five years in the UK have a history of foundering because of inadequate financing or lack of political will, largely as a result of the economic implications of such moves. So provision in the UK has grown piecemeal, and includes a wide range of different settings, including private and voluntary providers of day care, nursery schools, nursery classes attached to primary schools, Foundation Stage units, family centres, and, recently, integrated services delivered through Sure Start and children's centres which include nurseries. In order to orchestrate the development of provision in the late 1990s, the government required all local authorities to bring together providers of childcare and education through Early Years Development and Childcare Partnerships (EYDCP). Bringing together representatives of all providers was intended to promote better quality and more wide-ranging childcare services, as the EYDCP were able to approve finance for settings provided the staff met minimum standards of relevant qualifications. It raised local awareness and led to more coherent provision in some areas.

The notion of integrated services, bringing together care and education for young children and their families, which will be considered in greater detail in Chapter 2, has been largely perceived as being driven by the *Every Child Matters* Green Paper (DfES, 2003), and the subsequent Children Act in 2004. Yet such notions were at the heart of the 1994 Start Right Report. In his five major findings and 17 recommendations, Sir Christopher Ball stated unequivocally that young children were not only entitled to high-quality early education, but that such provision should be provided through a 'triangle of care', among parents, professionals and the community (1994, p7).

> *The Government should immediately prepare legislation to create by 1999 a statutory responsibility for the provision of free, high-quality, half-day pre-school education for all children from the age of three, in an integrated context of extended day-care. (Recommendation 12) (1994, p77)*

The Start Right Report acknowledged the importance of effective parenting for young children's early learning and development, and indeed the 'triangle of care' would allow parents to be supported by professionals in parenting their children.

The Start Right Report also emphasised other important themes in early learning and care. It put forward the suggestion that compulsory full-time education should begin at the age of six rather than five years, and that the money saved should be used to implement a system offering half-day early learning for all children aged between three and five years in an integrated setting. Read the extract below and reflect upon the main points which emerge.

EXTRACT ONE

Ball, C. (1994) **Start Right: The importance of early learning,** *RSA, Findings, pp75–6*

Findings

8.6 *From the review of the issues arising from a study of the importance of early learning, the nature of good practice and the search for a strategy of change, there arise five major findings. The first is the recognition that children's early learning, typically associated with the years three to six, forms a distinct and fundamental phase of education. It is not an 'optional extra', but a necessary foundation for successful schooling and adult learning. It has its own proper curriculum – which is distinct from, and preparatory to, Key Stage 1 of the National Curriculum. Those nations (like the UK) which have constructed a system of public provision for education which conceals or neglects this early learning phase have created a defective public understanding of the nature of good educational development. Good houses require strong foundations. A well-educated society needs nursery schools.*

8.7 *The second major finding is the importance of the triangle of care. There is a threefold responsibility for ensuring that every child enjoys a secure, warm and stimulating childhood. Parents, professionals and the community as a whole must work together in partnership since no one of them can be fully effective on their own. While each of these partners has their own proper role, they share a common purpose. Just as the medical profession in all its diversity is united in its aim to 'cure sometimes, relieve often, comfort always' – so the partners in the triangle of care need to come together in a common purpose to 'restrain sometimes, encourage often, love always'.*

8.8 *The third finding relates to quality. Both the evidence of research and the experience of other countries confirm the over-riding importance of high-quality provision for early learning. The ten common features of good practice are already well established in the UK, but need to be systematically applied and guaranteed through new arrangements for quality assurance.*

8.9 *The fourth major finding is that it is indeed possible for the UK to ensure that 'no child born after the year 2000 should be deprived of opportunity and support for effective early learning'. The resources required can be found. What has been lacking up to now is political will. This report has sought to demonstrate that investment in good early learning provides a worthwhile economic return. It has also argued that pre-school education should be recognised as a national priority. And it has suggested that even within a fixed educational budget, the relative value of nursery education is such as to justify a rebalancing of resources in favour of early learning. But the new approach outlined in Chapter 7 offers a way forward which is not only educationally attractive and cost effective in itself, but also designed to persuade even those who are unmoved by the arguments from investment, priorities or relative value. In such circumstances failure to make progress now would be a national disgrace.*

8.10 *And the fifth finding of this report is that in any event the current situation is little short of a national scandal. We have neglected the needs of the most vulnerable members of society – young children (especially those from deprived or disadvantaged backgrounds). Twenty-two years ago Margaret Thatcher saw what was required and published a White Paper which accepted the principle of nursery education. Governments of both the left and the right have subsequently abandoned the principle. For nearly a generation large numbers of the nation's children have been deprived of the right start to their lives, and society has paid the price in terms of educational failure and waste, low skills, disaffection and delinquency. Although remedial education for young people and adults can mitigate the damage, nothing can be done to retrieve the lost benefits of good early learning either for those who have missed it, or for the society which has neglected its responsibilities and wilfully overlooked the value and importance of providing all children with the right start. But we can do better in future.*

Issues raised include the following:

- *The importance of early learning;*

- *The recognition that what happens between the ages of three and six years forms a distinct phase of education;*

- *The notion of the triangle of care;*

- *The importance of quality in early years provision;*

- *The importance of political will;*

- *Provision has been a national scandal.*

Contrast these with the central principles of the government's ten-year strategy:

- *The importance of ensuring that every child has the best possible start in life;*

- *The need to respond to changing patterns of employment and ensure that parents, particularly mothers, can work and progress their careers;*

- *The legitimate expectations of families that they should be in control of the choices they make in balancing work and family life.*

What differences did you find? How far did the Start Right Report prepare the way for the government's policy on Early Years care and education? It is clear that the political drivers for the new Labour government were very much focused on employment of parents and opportunities for 'choice' about childcare. Issues of providing quality for children are embedded within the statement about 'children having the best possible start in life'. However, the importance of quality in childcare was not entirely neglected.

Karen's baby, Ben, is three months old. Karen is due to return to her job when Ben is six months old. She has been looking at possible childcare options. One option is the local private day nursery, part of a chain of private nurseries, fairly close to home, where Karen could leave Ben between 8.00 and 6.00 p.m. each day. The nursery is bright and colourful. Each child has their own key person who is responsible for build-ing a close relationship with a small group of children, and ensuring awareness of their needs. The staff at the day nursery are friendly and helpful, but changes of staff are frequent, which impacts negatively on the key person practice. A place at the day nurs-ery costs £175 a week. Another option is a local childminder who cares for a small number of children in her home, and who is part of a childminding network. The facili-ties in the childminder's house are those of a well-equipped home. The childminder charges £5 an hour and takes children between the hours of 8 a.m.and 6 p.m. As

> **SCENARIO** *continued*
>
> *Karen lives in a city, there is a new Sure Start children's centre due to open shortly. This will offer a day nursery, amongst other facilities combining childcare and education.*
>
> - *If you were Karen, what questions would you want to ask of each setting?*
>
> - *How would you decide upon the right setting for Ben?*

There are many concerns for parents looking for childcare and education for their children. Parents are eligible to apply for Child Tax Credit and Working Tax Credit, both of which are means-tested. The latter is targeted at parents who have children, and have low or middle-range incomes. It can be used towards childcare costs, but only with 'approved' childcare, which doesn't include anyone, such as a relative, who is not registered with the local authority. Consult the following websites for further information.

www.childcarelink.gov.uk/index.asp
www.bbc.co.uk/parenting/childcare/paying_workingparents.shtml
www.direct.gov.uk/en/Parents/Childcare/index.htm

The cost of childcare is certainly an important issue, as is accessibility, but the quality of that care is also crucial. The government acknowledges the issue of quality in its Ten Year Strategy, published in 2004. The importance of parenting is acknowledged (para 2.14), and quality of interaction is cited, although alongside more formal activities. The importance of the close relationship between parents and child, however, is not made explicit.

Nonetheless, evidence drawn from the Effective Provision of Pre-School Education project (EPPE, 2004), a longitudinal study of pre-school care and education, and other relevant research from the National Institute for Child Health and Development is used in support of the need for quality provision.

> **EXTRACT TWO**
>
> ### *DfES (2004) Choice for parents, the best start for children: a Ten Year Strategy for Children, HMSO, paras 2.13–2.21*
> *http://www.everychildmatters.gov.uk/_files/C7A546CB4579620B7381308E1C161A9D.pdf*
>
> **Child development**
>
> **2.13** *There is an increasingly rich evidence base concerning the factors that influence child development and, in particular, on how the experience of a child in the early years can have life long consequences.*
>
> **The importance of parenting**
>
> **2.14** *Parents and the home environment will always have the most important impact on a child's development. Where parents are actively engaged in activities with their children, they demonstrate better intellectual, social and behavioural development. Activities such as reading with children, teaching songs and nursery rhymes, drawing and playing with letters and numbers, all have a positive impact on children's intellectual and social development. The*

quality of these interactions between parents and their children is more significant for child outcomes than parental income or social background. However, evidence suggests that parents living in poverty are likely to face risk factors that make their role as parents harder, such as lack of material goods like toys and books, lack of space for play and school work, as well as a greater vulnerability to depression and anxiety.[1]

The first year of a child's life

2.15 *The evidence confirms the value of consistent one to one care in the first year of a child's life. In the early months there are health reasons, such as breast-feeding, that argue for a mother offering the best care. In addition, a number of studies suggest that full-time maternal employment during the very early stages of a child's life can have some small negative effects on the develop-ment of some children. However, these negative effects tend to be concentrated on full-time employment and can be avoided by high quality care from others and by an increased involvement of fathers.*

Age 1–3

2.16 *Evidence on child development between the ages of one to three shows that the impacts of childcare are mixed and sensitive to a variety of factors, the most important being the quality of care. Evidence from the National Institute for Child Health and Development (NICHD)*[2] *Early Child Care Research Network suggests that good quality care can boost cognitive skills and language. Evidence from the Effective Provision of Pre-school Education (EPPE)*[3] *project shows an early start to pre-school can have significant positive effects on chil-dren's cognitive and social development. For example, every additional month of quality pre-school from the age of two improves cognitive performance at the start of school, a gain that remains to at least age seven. Those who started in a good quality pre-school at two or younger were up to 10 months ahead of those without pre-school. The EPPE evidence also shows that an early start in pre-school improves children's social skills at entry to school. However, the studies indicate that high levels of group care of poor quality below the age of three can have a small negative effect on behaviour for some children.*

The impact of quality early education on 3–4 year olds

2.17 *The evidence shows that involvement in high quality early years education from age two onwards can lead to better educational and social outcomes for all chil-dren. Any pre-school experience can have clear positive effects on children's social, emotional and cognitive development. Evidence from EPPE shows that the benefits are gained from regular part-time attendance through the week. Full-time atten-dance gives no better gains than part-time although EPPE suggests that pre-school experiences at all levels of quality and duration have positive effects on children's development compared with children who had no pre-school experience.*

---

[2] The NICHD Early Child Care Research Network (2005) Child Care and Child Development, Guilford Press.
[3] Sylva, K., Melhuish E., Sammons, P., Siraj-Blatchford, I. and Taggart, B. (2004) The Effective Provision of Pre-school Education: final report Nottingham: DfES publications.

School age children

2.18 *There is also evidence to suggest that childcare for school age children can produce improved outcomes for pupils and the wider community. Evidence from the evaluation of extended schools indicates that wrap-around childcare and services have the potential to improve educational attainment and behaviour and increase parental involvement.*

Early education and childcare can help tackle disadvantage

2.19 *Participation in high quality group early years settings from the age of two can help children from disadvantaged backgrounds make up ground with their peers. For example, evaluation from the Early Head Start programme from the USA, which targets young disadvantaged children, found significant positive effects of high quality childcare for both child development and parental well being. EPPE also shows the relative gain for disadvantaged children is greater as they are starting from a lower base. Children from disadvantaged backgrounds benefit particularly from care in groups made up of a wide range of children, suggesting that there are social gains from ensuring that children attending a group setting come from a range of backgrounds.*

2.20 *While not wholly eliminating the impact of disadvantage, quality pre-school education can provide children from lower income households with a better start at school. EPPE data suggest that while one in three children were 'at risk' of having special educational needs at the start of pre-school, that proportion fell to one in five by the time they started primary school, suggesting that pre-school can be an effective intervention for the reduction of special needs.*

Implications for policy

2.21 *The evidence on child development has significant implications for policy. Most importantly it tells us that government involvement in childcare provision cannot be limited to securing adequate supply to support labour market participation. Government needs to care about the quality of childcare. The longer term benefits of getting the early years right will pay dividends both for individuals and for society as a whole as children grow to adulthood. More specifically the evidence suggests that:*

- *for the first year of a child's life the priority should be to create conditions that support consistent one to one care;*

- *for children aged one to three the priority for childcare must be high quality provision for those who choose to use it; and*

- *for children aged three and above regular participation in high quality group childcare can have a positive effect on cognitive, social and emotional development, and help support higher educational attainment in school.*

POINTS TO CONSIDER

• What do we mean by quality in Early Years settings?

• What does the reading suggest results from poor-quality early education and care?

• In what ways do quality pre-school education and care benefit children?

Curriculum issues

One way of trying to define and enhance quality is by providing a curriculum which guides the content and structure of the activities in which young children are engaged in their settings. In an Early Years curriculum, the content in the UK has traditionally been based around the ten principles of childhood (see Bruce, 2004), and prior to the introduction of the National Curriculum all providers were able to devise and implement their own curriculum. In a paper published in 1988, a number of Early Years specialists, calling themselves the Early Years Curriculum lobby, met with the Under Fives Unit at the National Children's Bureau to form the Early Years Curriculum Group. Their meetings resulted in the publication of a document entitled *The Early Years Curriculum and the National Curriculum (1989)*, which demonstrated how a play-based curriculum, responding to children's individual needs, could dovetail with the demands of the National Curriculum. However, partly because of the splintered nature of Early Years provision in the UK, and the consequent perception of pockets of poor-quality provision, and partly because of downward pressure from teachers in Key Stage 1 and above, the Conservative government in 1996 introduced an outcome-focused curriculum, with the title of *Desirable Outcomes for Children's Learning on Entry to School*, under six areas of learning. This was superseded in 2000 by the *Curriculum Guidance for the Foundation Stage*, a more accessible and appropriate document, which provided clearer guidance for practitioners to be able to support children individually and appropriately. But both these documents were focused on children between the ages of three and five years. What of those children under three years of age in day care settings? The development of the Birth to Three (2002) curriculum was intended to provide support and structure for this. The Birth to Three curriculum recognised children as strong active learners, and provided practical guidance in four areas of young children's learning and development.

The introduction of the new Early Years Foundation Stage (2007) is intended to bring together these two documents, and to improve quality across the Early Years sector. Issues about curriculum will be dealt with in detail in Chapter 8.

Responses to the curriculum documents have been varied; Physick (2005), for example, presents an interesting discussion of practitioner responses to policy change.

Qualifications issues

One of the problems resulting from the splintered provision in the UK is the lack of career options for those working with young children and families. Political and economic decisions made in the 1960s and 1970s, but camouflaged as welfare decisions, stated that children under five were best at home with their mother, and effectively undermined the development of coherent and comprehensive nursery education. The piecemeal development of provision, in response to parental need, had to be low cost to be affordable. In order to be affordable, staffing and resources costs had to be kept to a minimum. Opportunities for high-quality provision were therefore always going to be a challenge. Working with young children was not perceived as a viable career, and many of those diverted into working with children had few other options. The level of qualifications for those working with young children was often lamentably low, except in maintained nursery schools and classes, which employed qualified Early Years teachers and nursery nurses, whose nursery nurse qualifications were equivalent to A-level standard. In private day care, most practitioners hold qualifications at level 2 or level 3, and some are unqualified. Pay is poor and career opportunities limited. Contrast this with some of our European neighbours, for example Sweden, where, as long ago as 1999, according to Cohen *et al.* (2004), more than 50 per cent of Early Years practitioners had professional qualifications.

Evidence from the EPPE project demonstrates that the most effective and high-quality Early Years settings are those that offer integrated care and education, and which employ a qualified teacher. The OECD indicators of quality across European Early Years settings (2005) cited aspects such as ratios, space, the curriculum, staff training and qualifications.

Despite the government's intentions to improve quality and accessibility of affordable childcare, it is clearly a challenging task. In attempting to deal with low qualification levels, money has been diverted through the EYDCP to support training for those working in settings, aiming to ensure that all settings have a higher proportion of staff qualified to at least level 3 by 2008. But qualifications at levels 2 and 3 are considerably different to holding a professional qualification at degree level. The introduction of Early Years Foundation degrees, leading to the title of Senior Practitioner, was intended to establish further rungs in the 'climbing frame' (Abbot and Moylett, 1999) of qualifications for Early Years practitioners. Yet within the first two years that such Foundation degrees had begun the notion of Senior Practitioner in Early Years had been forgotten by the DfES. The introduction of the new Early Years Professional Status, equivalent to Qualified Teacher Status, and requiring similar entry qualifications, is another attempt to improve qualification levels in the Early Years sector. Early Years professionals are intended to lead practice for the new Early Years Foundation Stage curriculum (2007) which brings together the Birth to Three and the current Foundation Stage.

But levels of qualifications are not the most important issue for many parents who simply seek to find any appropriate care for their children.

Ball, S.J. and Vincent, C. (2005) New Labour, social justice and the childcare market, *BERJ, 31, 5, 558–560 (extracted from 557–570)*

New Labour childcare policy

Until the advent of the 1997 Labour government childcare was indeed a neglected area of public policy. As Denise Riley (1983) has noted, 'the very term "childcare" has a dispiriting and dutiful heaviness hanging over it ... it is as short on colour and incisiveness as the business of negotiating the wet kerb with the pushchair' (cited in Brennan, 1998, p. 3). However, the rising number of mothers with small children who were returning to the labour market was a phenomenon that demanded a response.[3] In addition, and importantly, early years care and education is a productive area for New Labour as initiatives here can theoretically address several agendas: increasing social inclusion and in particular combating child poverty, revitalising the labour market, and raising standards in education. The provision of childcare is seen as having the potential to bring women back into the workforce, thereby increasing productivity as well as lifting families out of poverty, modelling child-rearing skills to parents understood as being in need of such support, and giving children the skills and experience they need to succeed in compulsory education. It is worth noting, however, that these different agendas are only partially complementary.

Until recently, and as is the case in the USA (Uttal, 2002), the private sector has been the major beneficiary of the increasing number of women returning to work. In the period between 1990 and 2000 the UK day nursery market quadrupled, and day nurseries account for about 30% of registered child care places. The day nursery market is worth £2.66 billion (Blackburn, 2004) and in 2003, grew by 13%. The sector is currently experiencing a period of mergers and acquisitions among the larger operators, with Nord Anglia buying two other major but struggling chains, Leapfrog and Jigsaw, in 2004, making it the market leader in terms of size. Asquith Court, the former market leader, and kidsunlimited also announced a merger over the summer of 2004 to form the Nursery Years Group. However, this was then called off as being 'commercially unviable' (statement from kidsunlimited, reported in Nursery World, 11 November 2004). Despite this, more mergers and acquisitions are likely to follow, resulting, eventually, in perhaps three or four major players dominating the market, paralleling the history of the residential care sector (although independent small businesses are unlikely to completely disappear). However, at the moment the private day nursery sector remains a competitive, fragmented market. Currently, private sector providers outside London are complaining that their viability, in a period of falling birth rates, is further at risk from government funded Sure Start initiatives scooping up the limited numbers of children and staff in particular localities (Vevers, 2004a). Blackburn's 2004 report also notes a rise in vacancy rates nationwide for the second year running (Blackburn, 2004).

Through the National Childcare Strategy (Department for Education and Skills [DfES], 1998) and the new Ten Year Strategy (Her Majesty's Treasury [HMT], 2004), New Labour is committed to 'a longer term vision of the childcare market in which every

parent can access affordable, good quality childcare' (Baroness Ashton, DfES, 2002, cited in Mooney, 2003, p. 112, also HMT, 2004, p. 1). This is to be achieved through a plethora of initiatives, particularly directed at disadvantaged areas and lower income families. However, the rhetoric is increasingly of universal childcare (Vevers, 2004b; Labour Party, 2005), with services being provided through Children's Centres (integrated services on one site eventually planned to be in every local community, but initially in the most disadvantaged areas). The pace of expansion quickened markedly in 2004. As part of the Spending Review, the Chancellor announced in the summer of 2004 that 2500 Children's Centres will be open by 2008, and the 2005 manifesto promises 3500 Children's Centres by 2010 ('a universal local service' [Labour Party, 2005, p. 75])[4] The DfES five-year plan published in 2004 (DfES, 2004) also talks of a vision of integrated 'educare', with services available to families from 8 a.m. to 6 p.m., 48 weeks of the year. The emphasis is clearly on one-stop provision, drawing together a range of health, education and welfare and care services available eventually to all families. (There is, of course, a considerable body of literature on the difficulties of inter-agency collaboration. For one recent review, see Campbell & Whitty [2002].) The umbrella for these many projects is Sure Start[5], which now incorporates Children's Centres and the Neighbourhood Nurseries Initiative (designed to bring affordable care to disadvantaged areas). The future of Sure Start is contested (see Glass, 2005; Hodge, 2005) but local programmes will be wound up within the next two years as Children's Centres appear. Glass (2005) asserts that 'little [of the philosophy and ways of working] will remain but the brand name'.

The recently-published Ten Year Strategy (HMT, 2004) announced Labour's key proposals. The strategy takes account of earlier criticisms that Labour's plans were directed primarily at adult workers rather than children, by emphasising the benefits of pre-school education for children, and acknowledging 'a policy that gives too much emphasis to helping parents work could come at the expense of the needs of children' (HMT, 2004, para. 2.4). The strategy lays out plans for the extension of paid maternity leave to nine months from 2007 with a planned extension to 12 months by 2010. Some of that leave may be transferable to fathers. Children's Centres should number 3500 by 2010 (one in every 'community'), although they will be at their most numerous and most extensive in disadvantaged areas. Three- and four-year-olds will receive a phased extension of their free provision up to 15 hours per week (for 38 weeks a year) by 2010, with an ultimate goal of 20 hours per week. There is no mention of universal provision for one- and two-year-olds, however.

New Labour has also made tax credits available to lower income families, and from April 2005 an extension was announced of the childcare voucher scheme to offer working parents in participating companies income relief on the first £50 they earn each week. With regard to planning provision and ensuring well-trained staff, local authorities have been given the role of developing and supporting local provision. There will be a Transformation Fund from 2006 which will contain £125 million to 'help raise quality and sustainability'. A new training and qualifications structure is already being planned. An increase in Child Tax Credit will be introduced, and £5 million is to be invested in pilot schemes in London in recognition of the capital's particularly high childcare costs.

There are many praiseworthy government initiatives here. The Chancellor, Gordon Brown, was hailed as a 'childcare champion' in March 2004 by the pressure group and childcare charity the Daycare Trust. This was in response to the 2004 Budget, which directed increased spending of £669 million on early years education and childcare by 2008, and the July Spending Review, which saw an extra £100million for the development of Children's Centres. Thus, the Sure Start budget will rise by 17% in real terms from 2004/05 to 2007/08.

Nonetheless, there has been concern expressed by those in the field that the expansion which seeks to improve access to care has not been entirely thought through, although, as we note above, the Ten Year Strategy clearly seeks to address some campaigners' concerns. Writing just after the publication of the strategy, it seems that the following concerns (expressed in summer 2004) are still pertinent. A special report in the practitioner journal, Nursery World, *described the aims of the Spending Review and the five-year education plan as 'laudable' but also noted 'concerns over the level of funding, the absence of clear mechanisms for delivery, a perceived yawning gap in staff training and an unrealistic timescale' (Vevers, 2004c, p.10).[6]*

- *Think about the challenges that present themselves currently for private and voluntary day care providers.*

- *How far is the childcare strategy aimed mainly at adults rather than children?*

- *Review your original list of contexts in which children may be cared for and educated outside the home. Are there any others to add?*

In many ways, the radical changes of the past ten years continue to reverberate across the sector. The government's intention to have 2,500 children's centres by 2008 and 3,500 by 2010 has both posed a tremendous challenge for both local authorities and practitioners, and presented an opportunity to transform local services. The vision includes an Early Years professional in each children's centre, qualified to lead on Early Years curriculum practice. In this way, the government aims to promote quality affordable childcare and education.

A further aspect of policy is the creation of a Children's Commissioner for each of the four countries of the United Kingdom. The United Nations Convention on the Rights of the Child (UNCRC) was ratified by the UN in 1989, and emphasises that rights belong to all children without exception, and that children's best interests must be a prime consideration in all situations (www.unicef.org.uk/tz/rights/convention.asp). Building upon the UNCRC, agreed in the UK in 1991, and acknowledging the status of children as individuals who are entitled to be heard and treated with respect, the Office of the Children's

Commissioner has the task of ensuring that this is the case. The appointment of Professor Sir Al Aynsley-Green in 2004 as the first Children's Commissioner for England was unprecedented. The Childrens' Commissioner for Wales was appointed in 2001, and Northen Ireland Commissioner was appointed in 2003. There is also a Scottish Childrens' Commissioner who was appointed in 2004. Website addresses for the four commissioners are given at the end of this chapter. It is interesting to make comparisons between the different websites and the ways in which they present themselves to children, young people and adults.

The remit of the Children's Commissioners is very broad, but is within the five outcomes of the Every Child Matters framework, and concerned to 'look after the interests and act as the voice of children and young people'. The following web address provides a link to the home page of the English Commissioner aimed at an adult audience and provides an introduction to the Commissioner's work and a list of priorities.

https://www.childrenscommissioner.org/adult/index.cfm

It does seem that the role of Children's Commissioner offers an opportunity to focus on children's perceived needs and views rather than the views of the government and the adults around them as to what is appropriate for them.

The following extract is taken from the same website and highlights the views of children and young people on their perceptions of their needs which are presented both as an overview and also within specific age ranges.

EXTRACT FOUR

Office of the Children's Commissioner, Children and Young People's Plans: A Review of the First Year, November 2006

What Children and Young People told us they wanted

In this section, the views of children and young people, who were consulted as an integral part of this project, are represented. Approximately 200 children and young people participated directly in this project, adding their voices to this study. They collectively showed that despite variations in location, age or background, their priorities for change had much in common. Their priorities and hopes for their future, where possible, are presented in their own words and their views represented according to age group. Particular reference is made to children in care and disabled children who participated in a number of sessions.

In summary, children and young people consistently told us they:

- *Wanted to be free from bullying in their schools and communities;*
- *Would like their play areas to be safe, clean, with good lighting, and free from vandalism;*
- *Expected their views would be listened to and to be told what was the outcome of consultation and participation sessions; and*

- *Needed clear and unambiguous advice on sexual health, drugs and alcohol.*

Most of all, children and young people said they wanted:

- *To have fun, and be able to spend time with their friends and families in environments where they were safe and welcome.*

Age 0–5

Children in this age group were concerned about their immediate environment and the way it looked. They felt scared by things which made them feel unsafe, such as busy roads, glass, broken facilities and poorly kept parks and run-down houses. Even at this age, children were able to articulate what they liked and did not like. Things that were important to them were family, friends and having places to play at home and in school. They disliked their environment being spoilt by rubbish and graffiti and were able to identify ways of resolving their concerns with practical suggestions.

However, children who are very young will find it difficult to imagine solutions outside of their own experience. So, for example, a child who has never had access to adequate playing fields will need to be helped to think of possible solutions, aided by excursions, images, stories and examples to make it 'real'.

Children who were asked for their views about what would make their lives better made suggestions to improve play areas, including at school and in parks, increased road safety, and more comfortable homes generally ('my mum has new carpet so we don't get splinters anymore') this was particularly so for children who live in social housing or poor quality housing.

Age 5–10

Children in this age group told us they wanted to stop anti-social behaviour, and to feel safe playing in parks, particularly when older children shared their space as they were 'loafing about with nothing to do'.

The fear of older teenagers was a common theme, with many complaining that they had damaged their playgrounds with graffiti, intimidating them by drinking or smoking where they wished to play. Things that were positives were their families, friends and the knowledge that 'people care about you'.

'Bullying is bad ...'

'We want to help younger children ... we're worried about anti-social behaviour ... drinking and kids loafing around with nothing to do ... '

'They wind the swings up so we can't play and there's graffiti and rubbish and it looks bad.'

'Homes should be made better with more choice of colour and stuff ... '

https://www.childrenscommissioner.org/documents/report_las_cypp_ta_140806_1.01.doc

---

POINTS TO CONSIDER

- *Compare the websites of the four Commissioners. Which aspects are similar, and how do they differ? Which do you find most interesting?*

- *How far do you think young children are likely to be able to engage with the work of the Commissioners?*

- *How far do you think this development will make a difference to children's lives? It is worth bearing in mind the recent UNICEF report, in which the UK scored lowest in total of 21 developed countries across six measures of health, education and well-being.*

The true measure of a nation's standing is how well it attends to its children – their health and safety, their material security, their education and socialization, and their sense of being loved, valued, and included in the families and societies into which they are born.

(UNICEF, Child poverty in perspective, 2007)

However, the introduction of the Children's Commissioners appears to be a genuine opportunity to acknowledge and respect children as individuals, with views and priorities of their own.

C H A P T E R   S U M M A R Y

The aims of this chapter were to provide an overview of the tremendous changes which have occurred in Early Years and childcare over the past ten years, and to understand the policy-drivers which have been responsible for these changes. Further reading around this topic will give you a clearer and more in-depth understanding of these issues and their impact on young children and families.

REFERENCES

Abbot, L. and Moylett, H. (1999) *Early education transformed*. Abingdon: Falmer Press.

Ball, C. (1994) *Start Right: The importance of early learning*. London: RSA.

Bruce, T. (2004) *Developing learning in early childhood*. London: Paul Chapman Publishing.

Cohen, B., Moss, P., Petrie, P., and Wallace, J. (2004) *A new deal for children?* The University of Bristol: The Policy Press.

DfEE (1996) *Desirable outcomes for children's learning on entry before compulsory school age*. London: QCA.

DfEE (2000) *Curriculum Guidance for the Foundation Stage*. London: QCA.

DfES (2002) *Birth to Three Matters*. Sure Start.

Early Years Curriculum Group (1988) *Early childhood education*. Stoke on Trent: Trentham Books.

Early Years Foundation Stage documents can be found at **www.standards.dfes.gov.uk/eyfs/**

DfES (2003) *Every Child Matters* (Green Paper). London: DfES.

Elfer, P., Goldschmied, E. and Selleck, D. (2003) *Key persons in the nursery: Building relationships for quality provision*. London: David Fulton.

Physick, R. (2005) Changes and challenges: Pre-school practitioners' responses to policy change and development, in K. Hirst and C. Nutbrown, (eds) *Perspectives on early childhood education*. Stoke on Trent: Trentham Books.

Sylva, K., Melhuish, E., Sammons, P., Siraj-Blatchford, I. and Taggart, B. (2004) *The effective provision of pre-school education: Final report*. Nottingham: DfES Publications.

UNICEF (2007) Child poverty in perspective: An overview of child well-being in rich countries, *Innocenti Report Card 7*, 2007, UNICEF Innocenti Research Centre, Florence. © The United Nations Children's Fund, 2007. Full text and supporting documentation can be downloaded.

Early Years Foundation Stage documents can be found at **www.standards.dfes.gov.uk/eyfs/**

FURTHER READING

Baldock, P., Fitzgerald, D. and Kay, J. (2005) *Understanding Early Years Policy.* London: Paul Chapman.

Pugh, G. and Duffy, B. (2006) *Contemporary Issues in the Early Years* (4th edn). London: Sage.

WEBSITES

www.allchildrenni.gov.uk/index/commissioner.htm

www.bbc.co.uk/parenting/childcare/paying_workingparents.shtml

www.childcarelink.gov.uk/index.asp

www.childcom.org.uk/english/index.html (home page of the Children's Commissioner for Wales. These web pages are dual languages.)

www.childrenscommissioner.org

www.direct.gov.uk/en/Parents/Childcare/index.htm

www.everychildmatters.gov.uk

www.sccyp.org.uk/

www.unicef.org.uk/tz/rights/convention.asp

Chapter 2

Multiprofessional working

Helena Mitchell

Although the need for multiprofessional working has been clearly defined by policy initiatives in the past nine years, the establishment of the Every Child Matters agenda has added a further imperative to the agenda. This chapter will attempt to define these approaches, consider what they mean in practice, and what the implications are for those working with young children.

O B J E C T I V E S

By the end of this chapter you should have:
- considered definitions of multiprofessional working, and what this means in practice;
- an overview of the impact of the government's Every Child Matters legislation on professionals working with children and families, and on the children and families themselves;
- understood the policy imperatives which led to ECM;
- considered aspects of workforce development;
- critically evaluated the positive and negative aspects of the initiative.

Professional Standards for EYPS: S3, S4, S5, S6, S33, S36

Introduction

What do we mean by multiprofessional working? Work with young children and families has involved professionals from different agencies for many years. The birth of a baby automatically involves health care professionals, whilst social services may become involved at any time in a child's life. Until recently, the education service has not been involved with most children and families before children approach the age of five years, the statutory school starting age in this country. But with an increasing number of children attending nursery education, children beginning schooling from the age of four years in some areas, and the growth of private and voluntary day care providers, the overlap between different services has increased. There has been a move towards interagency working in children's services for some time, which can been seen in the establishment of the Early Excellence Centres in the late 1990s, charged with bringing together a range of provision for young children and families on one site. In actuality, many of the Early Excellence Centres were multi-sited, but they did succeed in bringing together elements of health, education and social work so that they were more accessible to families within local communities (Bertram and Pascal et al., 2002). Despite the apparent initial success of the Early Excellence Centres, they were overtaken by a further interagency initiative, Sure Start, and have now become Sure Start Children's Centres.

To return to the question posed at the beginning of this chapter, what is the meaning we ascribe to multiprofessional working? According to Atkinson et al. (2005), there are a number of different models which may include co-location of staff groups, the creation of new and separate structures, and the establishment of steering groups which drive forward change but possess no actual resources. Decisions are driven through the participants' organisations. Local area working is very important, with parents and carers involved throughout, so that services are responsive to local needs. The development of multiprofessional working may go through a number of stages, and Frost (2005) describes different levels of working, ranging from level one, which involves co-operation, through to level four, where there is total integration. Rowe (2005) discusses some of the challenges in a local Sure Start programme. See Chapter 4 for a discussion of health issues. The challenge of bringing together different services effectively is certainly a mammoth one, and issues of attitudes of the professionals involved are crucial to successful implementation. In addition, the need for effective communication by all participants has been identified by Glenny (2005) and Alexander and Macdonald (2001).

EXTRACT ONE

Cohen et al. (2004) A new deal for children? *Bristol: The Policy Press, pp8–9*

Consequently, the meaning is often unclear. A recent example of this is a Scottish Executive consultative document, Integrated strategy for the early years, *which presents 'a coherent vision of integrated services which together can meet the universal, and more individual needs of families and young children' (Scottish Executive, 2003b, para 2). Yet the document uses a wide range of other terms about the relationship between services: 'align', 'a coordinated and coherent framework', 'joined up working', 'working well together', 'joint planning, commissioning and single system service delivery', 'a single service', 'complementary role' and 'an integrated approach'. What is unclear is whether these are all considered synonymous with 'integrated' or indicate subtle shades of meaning about future relations between services.*

Even in the substantial academic literature on the concept of integration in various policy fields, the relationship between 'integration' and other concepts, such as 'coordination', is not clear. The US National Center for Service Integration, established in 1991, defined 'service integration' as a 'process by which a range of educational, health and social services are delivered in a coordinated manner to improve outcomes for children and families' (Ryan, 2003, p 36). In the field of social services, several authors have proposed a 'continuum of integration', starting with a minimal level of information sharing or awareness raising, then moving through various stages such as 'communication', 'cooperation' and 'collaboration' to full 'integration' or 'fusion' (Konrad, 1996; Ryan et al, 2002).

EXTRACT ONE continued

Specifically in the field of ECEC, and with a particular focus on decision making, Bradley (1982, pp 32-4) distinguishes 'eight aspects of coordination'. These ranged from 'dissociation' ('where sectors take a positive decision not to work with others'), through 'cooperation' ('working together towards a common end') and 'federation' ('separate sectors working together [with] each accepting the other's goal'), to 'unification' ('where services have a single administration'). However, Bradley notes that services administered by one department 'has not necessarily produced a unified service'.

We define 'service integration' as the extent to which services are merged or fused across a number of dimensions, both structural and conceptual. Structural dimensions include departmental responsibility, staffing, funding and regulation. Conceptual dimensions include principles, values, identity, approaches to practice, understandings of children and of learning, care and other purposes. Services, therefore, can vary from being totally integrated, as when previously separate services merge to become one, to being very partially integrated, as when, for example, they are the responsibility of one department and covered by the same regulatory regime but with little other signs of integration. Indeed, like Bradley, we would argue that being in the same department is not by itself enough to make services 'integrated'.

We would distinguish 'integration' from other concepts expressing closer relations between services. Services can be subject to measures that are intended to provide for closer and more effective working but fall short of integration. In these cases, perhaps, terms implying a more complementary approach between separate and distinct services, such as 'joined-up' working, coordination or collaboration, would be more appropriate and less misleading. Also, services may be partially integrated, for example by coming within the same departmental responsibility and regulatory framework, but remain distinct and therefore subject to efforts to promote closer working relations.

POINTS TO CONSIDER

- *Consider the different terminology used to define multiprofessional working. What does this mean to you?*

- *Working in a group, list the different ways in which you would need to liaise if you were working on a joint project.*

- *What measures would you take to improve liaison and make it more effective?*

It appears that multiprofessional working covers a wide range of different models of working, and the term itself has been chosen for use in this chapter because it relates to the workforce who are involved rather than to the agencies. It is the professionals who form the workforce who are required to work together. Ways in which the overarching government vision is translated into local versions of multiprofessional working are varied, and may not necessarily build upon already established partnerships in localities.

Every Child Matters and the establishment of Children's Trusts

The changes bringing together different agencies are underpinned by the five outcomes of Every Child Matters, which became law through the Children Act 2004, and has impacted not only on the professionals working with children and families but also on local and central government itself. The introduction of Every Child Matters is often cited as a response to the Laming Report on the death of Victoria Climbié in London in 2000, which in part it was. But it was also a fundamental part of the policy developments championed by the New Labour government since 1997, strengthening the provision for children and families through integrated working.

The Five Outcomes of Every Child Matters are:

Being Healthy   *good physical and mental health; living a healthy lifestyle*

Staying Safe   *protection from harm and neglect*

Enjoying and Achieving   *enjoying life and developing skills for adulthood*

Making a Positive Contribution   *positive involvement with society and community*

Economic Well Being   *able to achieve full potential, and not being hampered by economic disadvantage*

These outcomes must underpin work at all levels with children and families.

In addition the agenda is focused across the age range, and provision includes the establishment of extended schools as well as children's centres. The agenda is underpinned by major changes in local authorities where the establishment of Children's Trusts has been undertaken, as required by the Children Act 2004. The establishment of Children's Trusts has required the reconfiguration of leadership, administrative and support services in local authorities so that all those involved in working with children and families are also working in multidisciplinary teams, led by a Director of Children's Services. Each Children's Trust is required to have a Children and Young People's Plan (CYPP) to manage the delivery of integrated services.

Every Child Matters: Children's Trusts.
www.everychildmatters.gov.uk/aims/childrenstrusts

Children's trusts

Children's trusts bring together all services for children and young people in an area, underpinned by the Children Act 2004 duty to cooperate, to focus on improving outcomes for all children and young people.

They will support those who work every day with children, young people and their families to deliver better outcomes – with children and young people experiencing more integrated and responsive services, and specialist support embedded in and accessed through universal services.

People will work in effective multi-disciplinary teams, be trained jointly to tackle cultural and professional divides, use a lead professional model where many disciplines are involved, and be co-located, often in extended schools or children's centres.

Children's trusts will be supported by integrated processes. Some processes, like the Common Assessment Framework, will be centrally driven, whereas others will be specified at a local level.

While integrated delivery can be fostered in many ways, and at many levels, making sure the system overall is meeting the right needs for the right children and young people requires effective integrated strategies:

> *A joint needs assessment*

> *Shared decisions on priorities*

> *Identification of all available resources*

> *Joint plans to deploy them.*

This joint commissioning, underpinned by pooled resources, will ensure that those best able to provide the right packages of services can do so.

All of this requires arrangements for governance that ensure everyone shares the vision and give each the confidence to relinquish day-to-day control of decisions and resources, while maintaining the necessary high-level accountability for meeting their statutory duties in a new way.

Across the whole system there are some unifying features which help to link the various elements:

> *Leadership at every level, not just the director of children's services, but at the front line*

> *Performance management driving an outcomes focus at every level, from area inspection to rewards and incentives for individual staff*

> *Listening to the views of children and young people – on the priorities at a strategic level, and on how day-to-day practice is affecting them personally*

Sure Start

The growth in Children's Centres across the country focused initially on areas considered to be most in need of high-quality integrated services. These were mostly inner-city areas in large urban conurbations, and the focus was on families with children up to the age of four years. As the programme has been rolled out, however, all areas have been required to manage the development, and 3,500 Sure Start Children's Centres are in the process of being created across the country. This, of course, means that children and families should have access to social work, education and health which is local, accessible and located on one site where possible. This has required a massive building programme to update facilities as well as the relocation of professionals providing such services. The age range for the programme has been extended too, with a focus on young children up to the age of five years. A further addition to multiprofessional working is the development of the Extended School initiative, which involves schools developing a core offer of services including wraparound care and specialist services (**www.teachernet.gov.uk/wholeschool/ extendedschools/teachernetgovukcoreoffer/**).

Sure Start programmes have been the subject of a series of evaluations designed to provide clear evidence for further development, highlighting aspects of strength and areas needing reassessment.

Sure Start builds upon earlier integrated working such as Early Excellence and the Neighbourhood Nurseries initiative, which was completed in 2004 (**http://www.surestart. gov.uk/surestartservices/settings/neighbourhoodnurseries/**).

The name Sure Start is reminiscent of the Head Start Programme in the USA, and has similarities in that it is aimed at improving the social and cognitive development of children in low socioeconomic status (SES) areas. See **www.acf.hhs.gov/programs/hsb/** for further information about Head Start. But perhaps the most important recent research to underpin Sure Start is the *Effective Provision of Pre-School Practice* (EPPE), a longitudinal study which has examined the quality of provision for early education. One of EPPE's key findings was that quality was higher overall in integrated settings, nursery schools and nursery classes.

Sure Start is the epitome of the government's ambitions for integrated working, and it retains a leading role in the strategy for children and families. But there have been ongoing changes to its development and although it remains a government flagship, with developments continuing apace, the fundamental challenges around early years developments remain.

Norman Glass, who led the Treasury working group promoting the original Sure Start in 1998, highlighted the issue that Sure Start worked well as a local programme, but when the government determined it should be rolled out as a national programme and moved away from the local strengths, without substantial additional funding, this impacted on the success of the programme, particularly for those hard to reach families which Sure Start was essentially designed to target (**http://education.guardian.co.uk/earlyyears/ story/0,,1383617,00.html**).

Funding issues continue to challenge the effectiveness of the programme with revised budget allocations meeting increasing delivery requirements. As Glass states:

> *On childcare, we are in danger of heading towards a very British compromise – Scandinavian ambitions and British funding levels.*

(*Guardian*, 5 January 2005)

But overall, the creation of Sure Start is beginning to transform the ways in which early childcare and education are delivered. Planning guidance for the next phase of Children's Centres (2006–8) provides a vision of an increasing number of Sure Start Children's Centres, with a centre in each community, and 3,500 children's centres by 2010. The national evaluation of Sure Start provides a comprehensive range of information about the initial findings from the local and national programmes, and can be downloaded from **www.ness.bbk.ac.uk/** and provides comprehensive evidence about the effects on children and families. An in-depth study by Weinberger *et al.* (2005) which focuses on two local Sure Start programmes provides a fascinating range of evidence about many aspects of the programme. Some of the general findings from this study programme are contained in the extract below.

EXTRACT THREE

Weinberger et al. (2005). Learning from Sure Start, *Ch 19, Looking to the future, pp254 (ii)–256*

(ii) Whether the programme as a whole is more than the sum of its parts

There is some evidence that offering a combination of services within one programme has added to the value of all the services. There have been links between them. Parents using one service can be referred on to, or encouraged to take up, other services, for example, from the breastfeeding support scheme to baby massage or, for a parent with a sensory disability, from a language check to support to attend a mother and toddler group. If parents have a positive experience of one service, they are more likely to take up another if it is in the same familiar setting or obviously part of the same programme. It has been noticed that, as the programme has become more established, families who take up one service usually go on to more. It would have been very difficult to establish some services if others were not already established. Examples of this are the way in which a bereavement group grew out of the family support service, a teenage mothers' group developed out of the antenatal service, and a 'Play and Say' language scheme in toddler groups developed out of the 'talking check' service. Crèche provision has supported other services by freeing parents to participate. Services can share the same reception and secretarial infrastructure, database, and publicity. Every service has the potential to support every other service.

(iii) The impact on families

Previous chapters have described the impact of specific services on families, particularly on parents. What about the overall impact? Although research cannot yet tell us exactly how much impact there has been, with how many families, it is reasonable to conclude from studies in this book that to some degree children born in the Sure Start area are now less likely to have a mother smoking in pregnancy, less likely to be born below weight, less likely to be in poverty, less likely to be evicted, less likely to have an accident in the home, more likely to have been breastfed, more likely to experience good-quality out-of-home play and learning opportunities, more likely to have language delay identified and addressed, and more likely to have warmer and non-confrontational early relationships with their parents. Over and above this, staff who have worked with parents are convinced that many have gained enormously in self-esteem and confidence and that they have higher aspirations for their children as a result of engagement with the programme.

(iv) The area focus

An essential characteristic of the programme, in line with Sure Start policy, has been its focus on a clearly defined area. This has sometimes created difficulties, such as those discussed earlier in relation to out-of-area families wanting to use services. It has also been difficult on occasions to link with other agencies in primary care, social work and education whose own boundaries do not neatly map on to the programme area. It has been important to remember that families even in small geographical areas are heterogeneous and do not all have the same needs. On the other hand, within the programme there is strong support for the area focus. It is felt that the credibility of the programme in the eyes of the community, local loyalty to it, and even local pride in what has been accomplished individually and collectively depend upon the programme's association with a small locality. Also, from a practical point of view, having services within pram-pushing distances of families is very desirable. One member of staff commented, 'The message from people is that they want services that are local and accessible'. The area focus is welcomed by staff too. One said that it was good to be told, 'This is your patch'. Finally, it should be noted that for research and evaluation purposes it is very helpful to be able to define the population for a programme in geographical terms. Overall, we feel the advantages of having an area focus outweigh the disadvantages.

(v) The emergence of a new workforce

One of the most striking features of Sure Start is the way that workers from different agencies and professional backgrounds have been brought together to work towards a common aim. In addition, opportunities for paid work and volunteers, have been created. This has not been without difficulties. At first, the programme was not able to offer permanent employment contracts to staff (although it can now do so, subject to funding). Another issue relates particularly to the health professionals working for the programme. At the beginning they reported feeling isolated and marginalized by their peers, even if on secondment. The midwife in the pro-gramme could not be seconded; being employed to work in the programme meant that she lost her health employment status and was subsequently classified as a 'radi-cal and independent' practitioner, no longer able to remain a member of the Royal College of Midwifery. The community teacher's commitment to the programme and to the community distanced her from normal educational support services and promo-tion opportunities within the local education authority. One has to ask whether Sure Start is a professional opportunity or a professional cul-de-sac. An additional pressure on Sure Start professionals is that they feel they need continually to prove the worth of their work, unlike their counterparts in statutory agencies whose activities are not scrutinized in the same way. The only good thing that can be said about these difficul-ties is that they have had a bonding effect on programme staff.

Despite insecurities relating to employment, programme staff find the new Sure Start way of working rewarding. Different professional skills have been respected while, at the same time, professional boundaries have been broken down. For example, a social worker and a midwife have been able to work together with a group of teenage mothers before and after the birth of their babies; a teacher and a social worker have collaborated in parent education courses. Such collaborations would be difficult to sustain within statutory services. Professionals have had more opportunity to extend their work beyond the boundaries of their conventional roles and to respond flexibly to families' needs, for example a teacher working with parent groups, a midwife working on smoke cessation and breastfeeding, a social worker supporting families before children need the protection of outside agencies. This could have been difficult within statutory services. There is no doubt that the opportunity to work with families in these ways has kept staff within Sure Start. There is a widely held feeling that 'there's no going back' to the way they worked before.

POINTS TO CONSIDER

- *How successful was the combination of services offered in the Sure Start pro-grammes?*

- *How did the Sure Start programmes impact upon the families in the study?*

- *How was Sure Start perceived to be impacting upon the workforce?*

The impact on children and families

The ultimate intention of the move towards multiprofessional working is to benefit fami-lies and children. What impact is the development of multiprofessional working having on them? The vision is an excellent one which should provide an ideal opportunity for parents with young children who may find themselves isolated or unsupported.

One parent described her experience when moving to a new area in which a Sure Start local programme was operating:

> *We moved here a couple of months ago and didn't really know anyone. I was in the park one day with my two children, Joe who is five months and Tom who is two years, when I got chatting to another mum. She told me about this place and suggested it might be a good place to meet other families. I wasn't too sure but then I saw posters advertising the Sure Start Children's Centre and I thought I might give it a try. I went along to the Family Centre first which has a drop-in policy so we could go in and leave when it suited us. The staff were very friendly and we got to meet some other families which was good. There was also information about the other services on offer at the centre, and after a bit I thought I might try some of the others. So far I haven't but I know that there's a health visitor there and also a day nursery.*

POINTS TO CONSIDER

- In what other ways might the centre support the family?
- Why might some parents and children be reluctant to go to the centre?
- What could the centre do to attract hard-to-reach families?

Workforce development

Although the implementation of Every Child Matters has been supported by massive investment and a challenging programme of change, it may be that the most fundamental aspect requiring change has not been sufficiently included in this blueprint: that of the need for the development of the workforce. According to Moss (2006), the need for a pedagogical approach is clear. In drawing comparisons with the children's workforce in other countries, it appears that the notion of 'shared orientations and values' for the workforce from the beginning of their training is fundamental to success. Bringing together already established services with the difficulties of ensuring that all professionals have shared values and beliefs, and appreciate each other's viewpoints, is far more of a challenge.

The splintered nature of the Early Years workforce, with its varied range of qualifications and differing experiences, together with pay and conditions which lack uniformity, forms perhaps one of the major barriers to effective integrated working. The only exception to this is those working in the maintained education sector. Of those in the non-maintained sector, more than 50 per cent of those working with young children possess only level 2 qualifications, which is not even equivalent to A-level. To address this, the government introduced a new status in 2006; that of the Early Years Professional, a status (not a qualification) equivalent to Qualified Teacher Status. The role of the new Early Years Professional is to lead practice in the new Early Years Foundation Stage, which resonates with the government's aim of improving leadership at every level, as cited in the Children's Trusts document. The aim of ensuring that an Early Years Professional is in place in every Children's Centre by 2010, and every day care setting by 2015, is certainly part of this agenda. But the gap between the number of practitioners qualified to begin the EYPS, and the number working in EY centres who have only a level 2 or 3 NVQ (or even a lesser quali- fication) is huge. Ninety percent of practitioners in private and voluntary settings have qualifications which are below A-level standard. This issue was recognised by the govern- ment's Select Committee on Early Years as long ago as 2001, when Barry Sheerman, the Chair of the Select Committee, made the following point to the committee:

> *Most people in this country would not get someone who is unqualified and untrained to fix an appliance such as a washing machine or a dishwasher …*
>
> *However, many people leave their children in the care of unqualified people who are paid the minimum wage, or sometimes less when the rules are bent.*

(*Hansard*, 2001, 310WH)

The issues about the Early Years workforce have been recognised for many years by those working in the sector. The contrast between the qualifications, training and status of those working with children in the UK and in certain European countries is very marked. The drive towards integrated services in Sweden, for example, has been well ahead of that in England and Scotland (Cohen *et al.*, 2004). One way that this has been addressed in the UK has been through the development and growth of undergraduate courses in Childhood and Early Childhood Studies which have been introduced in universities and colleges since the mid-1990s with some of the first being led by social policy. The intro- duction of the degrees was driven academically by the recognition that too many of those working with young children lacked in-depth knowledge about child development, and that academic courses in childhood would enable the training of a new breed of profes- sional working with children, one who would be able to raise quality and would be entitled to better pay (Calder, 2006). Better quality would only be achieved by a better qualified but also more settled workforce. One of the major challenges for the Early Years private and voluntary sector is the high rates of staff turnover. There is a shortage of well- qualified and committed childcare professionals.

Partly to address this issue, the government's drive for a better qualified workforce has included the introduction of Foundation degrees, two- or three-year work-based routes for practitioners, sanctioned by employers, and forming part of a 'climbing frame' to enable childcare workers to move from the more usual National Professional Qualifications (NVQs) through to a full honours degree and the status of Early Years Professional, or even on to a PGCE course. The intention of these routes was initially to upgrade the qualifica- tion levels of practitioners but in many cases it has led to better qualified staff moving into areas of better provision for which they are now qualified. Such challenging issues in workforce reform reverberate across the sector.

The rapid changes in services and workforce requirements have created considerable chal- lenges as well as opportunities for the workforce. At present it is possible for practitioners to achieve both Qualified Teacher Status and Early Years Professional Status (although the latter is not currently funded for those who already hold QTS and work in a maintained school). Similar challenges are to be found for all those professionals involved in inte- grated working. In 2004, Moss described the current barriers between childcare workers and teachers as 'outmoded and an unsustainable two tier system', but this view does not seem to have been acceptable to the government.

EXTRACT FOUR

Anning, A. et al. (2006) **Developing multiprofessional teamwork for integrated children's services.** *Maidenhead: Open University Press, pp. 115–117*

Workforce reform for children's services

A second major central government initiative is the children's workforce strategy reform. A complex series of initiatives have been set up, with task groups and acronyms proliferating and changing at a dazzling rate – for example, the Modernization Agency (MA) and Development Agency (IdeA) leading to the Care Services Improvement Partnership (CSIP). At the time of writing this book a Children's Workforce Development Council (CWDC) had been set up, chaired by Estelle Morris, former Minister of Education. It is promised £15 million in government funding for 2006–7 and £30 million for 2007–8. However, this is a drop in the ocean when we consider the enormity of the task of retraining and initial training of the number of professionals needed to implement the integrated children's services agenda.

The CWDC is one of five bodies which make up the Care and Development Sector Skills Council. The CWDC represents workers in early years, educational welfare, learning mentors, Connexions, foster care and social care. It also coordinates the Children's Workforce Network (CWN), made up of organizations with responsibility for teaching and other school staff, child health staff, youth workers, youth justice workers and play workers. The CWDC is charged with developing a national workforce competence framework for all those working with children; though sadly the training of teachers to work with young children remains corralled within the deeply conservative Teacher Development Agency. The aim is to review national occupational standards and the current single qualifications frameworks. As the chief executive of CWDC argued: 'People will be able to see a career path upwards as well as across into other areas as they will see how their existing skills can be built upon and developed rather than starting from scratch' (Haywood 2005: 3).

There are massive dilemmas to be addressed in reforming the workforce for children's services. For example, in the early years workforce, delivering largely care services, more than half the personnel are not qualified beyond Level 2 (the equivalent of a diploma). In contrast, in schools 80 per cent of those working with under 5s are qualified at Level 4 (degree level) or beyond. There is a need to clarify the proliferation of qualifications in the field. We need to decide what all professionals working in children's services must know and be able to do. But we must also value specialisms and deploy specialist expertise strategically in the best interests of children and their families. So a qualification framework will need to include some core requirements but some key differences. In many ways, discipline differences in training programmes may be more taxing to conceptualize and design than the content and processes of qualifications across the disciplines of health and education. For example, how do you delineate, codify and assess core and specialist knowledge and skills for a health visitor working alongside a midwife or a teacher working in partnership with a classroom support assistant?

29

An extract from a report on the National Service Framework referenced above encapsulates the mood of workforce reform: 'Modernizing the way in which we meet the needs of children through changing roles and new ways of working [involves] the emphasis shifting from traditional professional boundaries to ensuring that the child's needs are met by someone with the right skills, whatever their job title or position in an organization' (DoH 2005a: 43).

Within the NHS a new contract for doctors and dentists has been implemented. A major programme of workforce review for other staff, 'Agenda for Change' prepared the way for a radical overhaul of working practices and pay. Social work training has been fundamentally reformed to move towards a graduate and registered profession, with bursaries provided for social work students (see www.gscc.org.uk).

Workforce reform will need to be accompanied by revised agreements on salaries and conditions. There is optimism in the rhetoric of political talk about upgrading the workforce for children's services. We have inherited a long tradition of low paid and undervalued staff delivering children's services. The resulting structural features of such services will be hard to redress. It will require a radical rethink in terms of how an upgraded work-force will be funded, at a national level.

But some progress is being made. For example, a ten-year strategy for childcare includes a transformation fund of £125 million per year to fund rising levels of pay as the qualifications and status of children's services professionals is upgraded. A new concept of 'an early years professional' is to be developed in the UK. This person may be a 'new' teacher trained to work across education and care settings catering from birth to 16-year-olds, or a 'pedagogue' of graduate status trained to work across the sectors of care, learning and health. The intention is that there will be an early years professional in all the 3500 Sure Start children's centres by 2010, in every full daycare setting by 2015 and in the long term in every birth to 5 foundation stage group setting.

There has been some attempt to address inequities in the school sector. Under the auspices of Raising Standards and Tackling the Workload *(ATL et al. 2003), classroom support workers in classrooms, nurseries and peripatetic teaching settings have been graded on criteria related to the job description of teaching assistant Levels 1 to 4. Levels and associated job specifications have clearly specified contractual numbers of weeks' pay. At Levels 1 and 2 staff are paid for term time only and at 3 and 4 for 52 weeks of the year. Teaching assistants are encouraged to progress through the levels and are to be offered associated training opportunities. For example, they may study for a two-year part time foundation degree, which will allow them access to Level 3 modules in undergraduate programmes to complete a degree programme. The foundation degree requires work placements or continuous employment so that worker competencies can be assessed by a mentor in the workplace, mostly using portfolios of evidence. Practitioners may then choose to apply for further training in postgraduate vocational qualifications, for example to train to be teachers or social workers.*

EXTRACT FOUR continued

Another central government strategy is to shift staff training for specialist roles into the budgets of employers. Increasingly, employers will be expected to support their staff who want to progress through various elements of training. Support may be direct, by financing additional qualifications, or indirect by offering practitioners day release to attend training programmes.

There are similar issues for workforce reform in the NHS. For example, as reforms are driven through in 2006 a major issue for CAMH teams is a new emphasis on evidence-based practice. NICE produced a number of clinical guidelines recommending evidence-based approaches to the management of problems such as depression, eating disorders and self-harm. The guidelines recommended specialist psychological interventions as being the treatments of choice; but this required a huge investment in training staff to deliver the treatments. At the time of writing this book it is unclear where the funding for this training is to come from.

Finally, the government has recognized the complexity of managing change within, the structural systems of children's services. This concern has led to introducing a graduate status National Professional Qualification in Integrated Centre Leadership (NPQICL). The scheme was piloted at the celebrated Pen Green Centre for delivering integrated services to young children and their families (Whalley and Pen Green Centre Team 1997) and was rolled out nationwide in 2005–6. The programme, established at master's level, provides a focus on leadership for a range of professionals co-located in integrated Children's Centres, and draws on a reflective practitioner model. This and other initiatives are intended to be pivotal to training leaders and managers to achieve sustainable, systemic change in children's services.

POINTS TO CONSIDER

- *Find out about The Common Core and the Common Assessment Framework. How are they intended to be used by childcare professionals?*

- *Consider whether those working together need to be able to take on different professional roles to some extent, or whether they need to have a clear understanding of each other's roles, and to support each other effectively.*

- *One way of developing an integrated workforce is to create training courses which have common elements for all those who are intended to become part of the children's workforce. Consider what the main elements of any such courses might be.*

It is clear that there is a need for commitment to shared working on the part of all those involved in multiprofessional contexts, but strong leadership (Chandler, 2006) with a shared vision and values, is also essential.

CHAPTER SUMMARY

The introduction of multiprofessional working is radically transforming the ways in which professionals work together, and the services they offer to children and families. There are many potential benefits resulting from this requirement, although it offers many challenges for the professional involved. This is a brave new vision, which has the potential to transform the services themselves, and the society they serve. But there are many challenges to be overcome before the vision is achieved.

REFERENCES

Alexander, H. and Macdonald, E. (2001) The art of integrated multi-disciplinary partnership working: are there people who just don't want to play? Paper presented at Scottish Evaluation society conference.

Anning, A., Cottrell, D., Frost, N., Green, J. and Robinson, M. (2006) *Developing multiprofessional teamwork for integrated children's services.* Maidenhead: Open University Press.

Atkinson, M. Doherty, P. and Kinder, K. (2005) Multi-agency working, *Journal of Early Childhood Research*, Sage Publications, 3 (1), 7–17.

Bertram, T., Pascal, C., Bokhari, S., Gasper, M., and Holterman, S. (2002) *Early Excellence Centre Pilot Programme Second Evaluation Report 2000–2001*, Research Report 361, DfES.

Calder, P. (2006) History and background of the Early Childhood Studies Degree Network. Unpublished paper produced for Early Childhood Studies Degree Network Conference, Research into Reality, Woburn House, London, 14 March 2006.

Chandler, T. (2006) Working in multidisciplinary teams, in G. Pugh and B. Duffy, *Contemporary issues in the early years* (4th edn) London: Sage.

Cohen, B., Moss, P., Petrie, P. and Wallace, J. (2004) *A new deal for children?* Bristol: The Policy Press.

Frost, N. (2005) *Professionalism, partnership and joined up thinking.* Totnes: Research in Practice.

Glenny, G. (2005) Riding the dragon: Exploring the principles that underpin effective interagency networking, *Support for Learning*, 20 (4), 167–175, November.

Hansard, 2001, 310WH.

Moss, P. (2006) Farewell to childcare?, *National Institute Economic Review*, N.195, January.

Moss, P. (2004) Why we need a well qualified early childhood workforce. Paper presented at The Early Years Workforce: A Graduate Future. Early Childhood Studies Degrees Network Conference, Regent's College, London, 16 March.

Rowe, A. (2005) The impact of Sure Start on health visiting, in J. Weinberger, C. Pickstone and P. Hannon, *Learning from Sure Start.* Maidenhead: Open University Press.

Weinberger, J., Pickstone, C. and Hannon, P. (2005) *Learning from Sure Start.* Maidenhead: Open University Press. **www.ness.bbk.ac.uk/**

FURTHER READING

Siraj-Blatchford, I., Clarke, K . and Needham, M. (2007) *The team around the child*. Stoke on Trent: Trentham Books.

WEBSITES

www.dfes.gov.uk.commoncore/

www.everychildmatters.gov.uk/deliveringservices/caf/

Chapter 3
The nature of learning

Mary Wild

This chapter will consider some different ways in which theorists have sought to explain how young children learn.

OBJECTIVES

By the end of this chapter you should have:
- considered the contribution to our understanding of learning of two major theorists: Piaget and Vygotsky, and will have reflected on the similarities and differences between their theories;
- reflected on the ways in which theoretical accounts may be critically evaluated and challenged over time;
- thought about whether learning is an essentially individual or social experience for children;
- considered the implications of different theories for your professional practice within the Early Years.

Professional Standards for EYPS: S2, S3, S7, S8, S9, S16, S17, S21, S22

As you read through this chapter think about your own experiences of learning, both as a child and as an adult. How do these experiences relate to the theories that you are reading about? If you have a role that involves working with young children, think about what sorts of learning experiences you provide for them. Again, how do these relate to the theories that are covered here? Have the confidence, too, to consider whether there are other factors that your experience tells you may be important for effective learning.

Introduction

If we are to be able to provide effective learning experiences for young children then we need to have an understanding of how children learn and develop. Without some theoretical understanding the danger is that, at best, we do things in particular ways out of professional habit and thereby run the risk of not providing as worthwhile a learning experience as we could. At worst we may continue with practices that could impact negatively upon the children's learning and well-being.

The importance of the learning opportunities we provide being based on a sound knowledge of children's developmental needs is something that underpinned both the Birth to Three Matters Framework (David et al., 2003) and the principles of the Curriculum Guidance for the Foundation Stage (QCA, 2000).

It continues to be foregrounded in the Standards for the new Early Years Professional Status (CWDC, 2007) and is a central element within the new Early Years Foundation Stage:

> *All practitioners should, therefore, look carefully at the children in their care, consider their needs, their interests, and their stages of development and use all of this information to help plan a challenging and enjoyable experience across all the areas of Learning and Development.*

(DfES, 2007, p11)

The pre-eminence of a developmentally appropriate approach to learning, driven in the main by theories from development psychologists, is not without its challengers (Penn, 2005). There is a legitimate concern that theories of learning and development that suggest universally applicable rules and processes may overlook the natural variation between individuals and the crucial importance of the societal and cultural context. The extracts that you will be introduced to in this chapter therefore range from those that offer a predominantly individualist account of learning to those that quite explicitly highlight the role of the social and cultural context. As you read through the extracts you will be invited to consider the strengths and limitations of each account and to form your own opinions.

In contrast to extracts in other chapters in this book, some of the extracts included in this chapter may seem quite old. This is quite deliberate, since they may be characterised as classic and seminal texts. If you are studying Early Childhood studies or similar subjects you will encounter innumerable references to these works and very many differing opinions . By presenting extracts from the original works it is hoped that you will feel confident to consider your own response to the ideas that are suggested, and may then feel more knowledgeable in critiquing the views of other authors and indeed in drawing out implications for your own practice.

As you read through the extracts you will notice that the first three are linked in that they demonstrate how theoretical understandings are progressively developed through a process of critical challenge and interrogation. Being able to recognise how ideas are developed in this way is a crucial skill for you to develop as a student of Early Childhood studies.

There is an extensive array of possible literature on children's learning and development and it would be impossible to cover it all within one chapter, but throughout the chapter you will find references to other theoretical accounts of learning and suggestions for further reading around these.

Setting the scene: What is effective learning?

We all have experiences of learning something new. Think about yourself as a learner as an adult and back to your own experiences of learning as a child. When did you learn best? Was it when you were active, motivated, interested in what you were learning? Do you learn best when left to your own devices to experiment and try things out? Do you learn better when you have others around you? How much guidance do you need to help you learn?

If you have experience of working with or caring for young children, what do you think helps them to learn? Do you think it comes naturally and actually you don't need to do very much or have you a more direct role to play in helping children to learn?

Is learning a passive or an active process?

Learning has not always been seen as an active process in which the learner actively makes sense of the environment around him/her. For much of the twentieth century psychological accounts of learning were dominated by the behaviourist school of thinking, that sought to describe a process of learning whereby the learner reacted to external stimuli and in the course of doing so over repeated occasions learnt to act in particular ways (Skinner, 1974). The external stimuli were conceived of as mechanisms for reinforcing particular actions on the part of the child which could act to positively reinforce the behaviour, i.e. ensure that it would be repeated, or to negatively reinforce the behaviour, i.e. ensure that such behaviour would not be repeated. It is a model of learning that is akin to that used in training an animal; with the trainer, or parent or teacher, shaping the behaviours of the child over time. The role of the child is essentially as a passive respondent to extrinsic reward or punishment. Examples of this approach to learning are still evident in professional practices today. Consider for example the practice of rewarding what is seen as positive behaviour with stickers/praise in the expectation that children will repeat such behaviour. Thinking of cognitive learning too, you will know of learning resources that adopt this underlying approach to learning such as some of the drill-and-practice type computer resources that are available to use in the home or classroom. You may be able to think of some other examples from practice.

What was missing from this account of learning was any sense of what was happening within the child during the learning and any account of the intrinsic motivation to explore and learn from the environment around him/her. The idea of a child being an active explorer and mental constructor of his/her understanding was a key insight provided by Piaget, the co-author of the first extract in this chapter.

In the first extract from Piaget and Inhelder the theoretical account of what happens mentally when learning is occurring quite obviously attempts to redress the limitations of the behaviourist approach.

This extract includes three key concepts;

- Schemas
  - Which are seen as the existing mental representation that the child has of a particular situation or experience
- Assimilation
  - Which is seen as the way in which the child assimilates or processes new information that is available. In effect, how does the new situation/experiences fit, or not, with what I already know?
- Accommodation
  - Which is seen as the way in which the child has to accommodate, or alter, their existing schemas to take into account the new situation/experiences. In effect, how do I now need to change what I know?

As you read the extract you may well find some of the language used quite dense and challenging. This can be the nature of some developmental texts but try not to be put off by this; adjusting to the different tenor and styles of academic writing is an important skill to practise. Ultimately if you become confident in reading such seminal texts yourself, you will be less reliant on received opinion and will become more confident in knowing why you do what you do in your practice.

Piaget, J. and Inhelder, B. (1966) The psychology of the child. *London: Routledge and Kegan Paul, pp.5–6*

For many psychologists this mechanism is one of association, a cumulative process by which conditionings are added to reflexes and many other acquisitions to the conditionings themselves. According to this view, every acquisition, from the simplest to the most complex, is regarded as a response to external stimuli, a response whose associative character expresses a complete control of development by external connections. One of us,[8] on the other hand, has argued that this mechanism consists in assimilation *(comparable to biological assimilation in the broad sense): meaning that reality data are treated or modified in such a way as to become incorporated into the structure of the subject. In other words, every newly established connection is integrated into an existing schematism. According to this view, the organizing activity of the subject must be considered just as important as the connections inherent in the external stimuli, for the subject becomes aware of these connections only to the degree that he can assimilate them by means of his existing structures. In other words, associationism conceives the relationship between stimulus and response in a unilateral manner: $S \rightarrow R$; whereas the point of view of assimilation presupposes a reciprocity $S \rightleftarrows R$; that is to say, the input, the stimulus, is filtered through a structure that consists of the action-schemes (or, at a higher level, the operations of thought), which in turn are modified and enriched when the subject's behavioral repertoire is accommodated to the demands of reality. The filtering or modification of the input is called* assimilation; *the modification of internal schemes to fit reality is called* accommodation.*

[8] Jean Piaget, The Origins of Intelligence in Children *(New York: International Universities Press, 1951; London: Routledge and Kegan Paul, 1953).*

- *In what ways could you organise learning opportunities in an Early Years setting such that children can actively explore their own environment?*

- *How would you ensure that the learning environment provides cognitive challenges for the children?*

- *In what ways does this account of learning fit with or challenge your own beliefs about learning and/or your experiences of helping children to learn?*

- *You may want to read about some other accounts of learning such as:*
  - *Those that suggest that different individuals may have different and preferential ways of learning, sometimes known as learning style theories (Honey and Mumford, 1992).*
  - *Those theories that use computer modelling techniques that seek to simulate and describe what is happening within the brain when we learn something new.*

Stages of development

A second important aspect to the work of Piaget was the notion that children progress through a series of linear stages in their development. In the short extract that follows the notion of a stage theory is neatly encapsulated. As you read it, note down what you think are the key features of such an approach to developmental theory.

EXTRACT TWO

Piaget, J. and Inhelder, B. (1966) The psychology of the child. *London: Routledge and Kegan Paul, p.153*

The integration of successive structures, each of which leads to the emergence of the subsequent one, makes it possible to divide the child's development into long periods or stages and subperiods or substages which can be characterized as follows: (1) Their order of succession is constant, although the average ages at which they occur may vary with the individual, according to his degree of intelligence or with the social milieu. Thus the unfolding of the stages may give rise to accelerations or retardations, but their sequence remains constant in the areas (operations, etc.) in which such stages have been shown to exist. (2) Each stage is characterized by an overall structure in terms of which the main behavior patterns can be explained. In order to establish such explanatory stages it is not sufficient to refer to these patterns as such or to the predominance of a given characteristic (as is the case with the stages proposed by Freud and Wallon). (3) These overall structures are integrative and non-interchangeable. Each results from the preceding one, integrating it as a subordinate structure, and prepares for the subsequent one, into which it is sooner or later itself integrated.

POINTS TO CONSIDER

- *What are the implications for practice of a stage theory of development?*

- *To what extent does your experience of working with children support the notion that development is a linear process, i.e. proceeding clearly from one stage to the next? Is there anything in your experiences that would cause you to question this?*

- *Consider the links of such theories to particular curriculum approaches such as the Developmentally Appropriate Practices approach (Bredekamp and Copple,1997) and within the Birth to Three framework, CGFS and the new EYFS.*

As was noted earlier, some authors (Penn, 2005) have challenged the hegemony of a Western-dominated model of child development that fails to account for the individually diverse ways in which development might actually proceed and the cultural assumptions implicit in looking for universally applicable goals of development. As Rogoff and Morelli (1989, p19) point out,

Human functioning cannot be separated from the cultural and more immediate context in which children develop.

Nevertheless, the notion that development may occur in a series of stages, as Piaget suggested, has popular credence and although the precise depiction of what develops and when may well be open to challenge, it possesses some intrinsic credibility when we consider children that we know or have worked with, or indeed our own experience of growing up. We can discern a pattern of becoming capable of doing things that we were unable to do when younger and we can sometimes see how an earlier ability, awareness or skill acts as a building block for later abilities. Exactly what develops and in what order is the core content of countless academic papers, textbooks, and guides for parents and practitioners.

Because of the plethora of sometimes conflicting information available it is important that as students and as practitioners in the Early Years you become confident in critically appraising the different sources of information that you will encounter. In this context it is instructive to return to the precise details of the stage theory that Piaget himself developed and to see how subsequent academic challenge served to redefine understandings of the level of development and capabilities of children, in particular those aged between 2 and 7.

Challenging Piaget

Piaget (1962) proposed that the intellectual development of the child proceeds through a series of four stages:

- Sensori-motor
  - Covering the infancy period to age 2*

    During which the child's cognitive development is driven by repetitive actions, movements and sensory perceptions.

- Pre-operational;
  - Covering the age period 2–7 years*

    During which the child begins to develop some symbolic representations that enable the child to internally represent his actions but he continues to reason on the basis of what he directly sees or encounters. The focus is on how things are actually configured rather than on any 'transformations' or logical sequences that might have occurred.

- Concrete operational
  - Covering the age period 7–12 years*

    During which the child begins to make logical and reversible connections about the world around him but only where these are supported by tangible or concrete and observable examples.

- Formal operations
  - From age 12 upwards*

    Only by this point does a child come to be able to reason hypothetically and in the abstract.

*NB *It is important to acknowledge that these are approximate age boundaries but the sequence is seen as fixed and the age ranges themselves are assumed to be widely applicable and generally appropriate.*

In the extract which follows the focus is on the second of these stages and interrogates Piaget's characterisation of this stage of learning in terms of what children of this age are unable to do. The extract focuses on one of the more well-known experiments that Piaget conducted in drawing up his theory and gives you an insight into how crucial the methodology underpinning a study can be in shaping the outcome. As you read the extract make a note of the specific methodological points that are raised by Donaldson. Ask yourself too whether her critique leads you to see learning as more of a social than an individualistic process.

EXTRACT THREE

Donaldson, M. (1987) Children's minds. *London: Fontana Press, pp19–24*

In recent years Piaget has collected most of his data by devising tasks for children to do and then observing their behaviour when they deal with the task, questioning them about it, noting what they say. One of the best known of these tasks is concerned with the ability to take account of someone else's point of view in the literal sense – that is, to recognize what someone else will see who is looking at the same thing as oneself but from the other side.

For this task, a three-dimensional object or set of objects is needed. Piaget uses a model of three mountains. (See The Child's Conception of Space *by Piaget and Inhelder.) The mountains are distinguished from one another by colour and by such features as snow on one, a house on top of another, a red cross at the summit of the third.*

The child sits at one side of the table on which this model is placed. The experimenter then produces a little doll and puts the doll at some other position round the table. The problem for the a child is: what does the doll see?

In one version of the task the child is given a set of ten pictures of the model taken from different angles, and he is asked to choose the one which shows what the doll sees. In another version he is given three cardboard 'mountains' and he is asked to arrange them so that they represent what would be seen in a snapshot taken from the doll's position. Children up to the age of around eight, or even nine, cannot as a rule do this successfully, and there is a powerful tendency among children below the age of six or seven to choose the picture – or build the model – which represents their own point of view – exactly what they themselves see.

Piaget takes this to indicate that they are unable to 'decentre' in imagination. He points out that in one sense they know perfectly well that the appearance of a thing changes when you walk round it. And yet he maintains that they are bound by what he calls 'the egocentric illusion' as soon as they are called upon to form a mental representation of some view which they have not actually seen.

But first let us consider how children perform on a task which is in some ways very like the 'mountains' task and in other extremely important ways very different.

This task was devised by Martin Hughes. In its simplest form, it makes use of two 'walls' intersecting to form a cross, and two small dolls, representing respectively a policeman and a little boy. Seen from above, the lay-out (before the boy doll is put in position) is like this:

In the studies which Hughes conducted the policeman was placed initially as in the diagram so that be could see the areas marked B and D, while the areas A and C were hidden from him by the wall.

The child was then introduced to the task very carefully, in ways that were designed to give him every chance of understanding the situation fully and grasping what was being asked of him. First, Hughes put the boy doll in section A and asked if the policeman could see the boy there. The question was repeated for sections B, C and D in turn. Next the policeman was placed on the opposite side, facing the wall that divides A from C, and the child was asked to 'hide the doll so that the policeman can't see him'. If the child made any mistakes at these preliminary stages, his error was pointed out to him, and the question was repeated until the correct answer was given. Ways that would help the children to understand the nature of the problem, but in fact his precautions were largely unnecessary: the children seemed to grasp the situation at once. We have then to ask why this was so easy for them.

Notice that we cannot appeal to direct actual experience: few, if any, of these children had ever tried to hide from a policeman. But we can appeal to the generalization of experience: they know what it is to try to hide. Also they know what it is to be naughty and to want to evade the consequences. So they can easily conceive that a boy might want to hide from a policeman if he had been a bad boy; for in this case it would be the job of the policeman to catch him and the consequences of being caught would be undesirable.

The point is that the motives and intentions of the characters are entirely comprehensible, even to a 'child' of three. The task requires the child to act in ways which are in line with certain very basic human purposes and interactions (escape and pursuit) – it makes human sense. Thus it is not at all hard to convey to the child what he is supposed to do: he apprehends it instantly. It then turns out that neither is it hard for him to do it. In other words, in this context he shows none of the difficulty in 'decentring' which Piaget ascribes to him.

- *To what extent does this imply that learning may be a fundamentally more social experience than Piaget allows for?*
- *What might be the implications of the notion of 'human sense' for practitioners in planning for the learning of young children?*

POINTS TO CONSIDER continued

- When looking at developmental theories, remember to be aware of how the studies have been conducted and to ask yourself how that might have impinged on the reported findings.

This is only one exemplar from Margaret Donaldson's book and you may find it useful to follow up by reading the book in its entirety.

Learning as a social experience

As you read through the previous extract you will have detected the underlying notion that social context and interactions may be an important factor in children's learning. Donaldson's focus is on the importance to the child of the social meaningfulness of the situation but has resonance with the theories of another seminal developmental theorist of the twentieth century. Vygotsky's work, though undertaken in the first half of the twentieth century in the USSR, only came to prominence within the West in the 1960s and 1970s. His principal idea was that a child actively constructs his own knowledge from his experiences of the world around him and that there is a crucial role in this for the social experiences and interactions of the child. There is a similarity to Piaget's ideas in the notion of the child actively constructing his/her knowledge but the key element that distinguishes the theorists is the prominence given to social interactions in this process. Within this account of learning Vygotsky introduced a new concept called the Zone of Proximal Development (ZPD) that helped to explicate the role of others in supporting and extending the learning of children. In the next extract this ZPD is described by Vygotsky.

The ZPD is a concept that you will find covered in very many textbooks and articles that offer accounts of learning and development. Like the works of Piaget, there is no shortage of such accounts, but as a critical student of Early Childhood it is important for you to read not merely second-hand accounts of these theories but to read the originals for yourself. In becoming a reflective student and practitioner the skill of going beyond received opinion and feeling empowered to engage directly with the works of the major theorists is a skill well worth developing.

As you read the extract from Vygotsky think about examples from your own experience or practice that suggest that the distinction between an 'actual developmental level' and a level of 'potential development' is indeed a valid one.

EXTRACT FOUR

Vygotsky, L.S. (1978) **Mind in society. The development of higher psychological processes.** *Cambridge, MA: Harvard University Press, pp85–87*

Zone of Proximal Development: A New Approach

The first level can be called the actual developmental level, *that is, the level of development of a child's mental functions that has been established as a result of certain already completed developmental cycles. When we determine a child's mental age by using tests, we are almost always dealing with the actual developmental level. In studies of children's mental development it is generally assumed that only those things that children can do on their own are indicative of mental abilities. We give children a battery of tests or a variety of tasks of varying degrees of difficulty, and we judge the extent of their mental development on the basis of how they solve them and at what level of difficulty. On the other hand, if we offer leading questions or show how the problem is to be solved and the child then solves it, or if the teacher initiates the solution and the child completes it or solves it in collaboration with other children – in short if the child barely misses an independent solution of the problem – the solution is not regarded as indicative of his mental development. This 'truth' was familiar and reinforced by common sense. Over a decade even the profoundest thinkers never questioned the assumption; they never entertained the notion that what children can do with the assistance of others might be in some sense even more indicative of their mental development than what they can do alone.*

Let us take a simple example. Suppose I investigate two children upon entrance into school, both of whom are ten years old chronologically and eight years old in terms of mental development. Can I say that they are the same age mentally? Of course. What does this mean? It means that they can independently deal with tasks up to the degree of difficulty that has been standardized for the eight-year-old level. If I stop at this point, people would imagine that the subsequent course of mental development and of school learning for these children will be the same, because it depends on their intellect. Of course, there may be other factors, for example, if one child was sick for half a year while the other was never absent from school; but generally speaking, the fate of these children should be the same. Now imagine that I do not terminate my study at this point, but only begin it. These children seem to be capable of handling problems up to an eight-year-old's level, but not beyond that. Suppose that I show them various ways of dealing with the problem. Different experimenters might employ different modes of demonstration in different cases: some might run through an entire demonstration and ask the children to repeat it, others might initiate the solution and ask the child to finish it, or offer leading questions. In short, in some way or another I propose that the children solve the problem with my assistance. Under these circumstances it turns out that the first child can deal with problems up to a twelve-year-old's level, the second up to a nine-year-old's. Now, are these children mentally the same?

When it was first shown that the capability of children with equal levels of mental development to learn under a teacher's guidance varied to a high degree, it became apparent that those children were not mentally the same age and that the subsequent course of their learning would obviously be different. This difference between twelve and eight, or between nine and eight, is what we call the zone of proximal development. It is the distance between the actual developmental level as determined by independent problem solving and the level of potential development as determined through problem solving under adult guidance or in collaboration with more capable peers.

> POINTS TO CONSIDER
>
> - *What are the implications of the ZPD for the role of the adult in an EY setting?*
>
> - *How might a practitioner facilitate productive peer interactions?*
>
> - *What are the implications of the ideas in the extract for testing and assessment in the Early Years?*
>
> - *The ideas of Vygotsky are closely related to the ideas of other theorists that you might like to follow up. In particular it would be useful to read the work of Bruner in relation to 'scaffolding' (Wood et al., 1976) and Rogoff regarding the concept of guided participation (Rogoff, 1990).*
>
> - *More recently the Effective Provision of Pre-school Education research project (Sylva et al., 2004) and the associated Researching Effective Pedagogy in the Early Years project (Siraj-Blatchford et al., 2002) have identified the notion of sustained shared thinking as a crucial element in effective practice within Early Years settings. Reading the EPPE and REPEY findings will help you to envisage the crucial role of social interaction in a very direct way.*
>
> - *Sustained shared thinking is defined within the REPEY report as: 'An episode in which two or more individuals "work together" in an intellectual way to solve a problem, clarify a concept, evaluate activities, extend a narrative etc. Both parties must contribute to the thinking and it must develop and extend' (p9). You may like to bear this in mind later in the Reader in Chapter 7, when the theme of sustained shared thinking is revisited in relation to play.*

Learning as a cultural process

Vygotsky's account of learning went further than purely ascribing a key role for social interaction in learning. He argued that the particular social interactions that take place, and the language and forms of communication that are used are themselves shaped and driven by the broader cultural context in which they take place, not just at the level of what you know but in terms of how your thoughts and concepts are formed. Hence the learning of an individual is a fundamentally social and cultural process.

This is not to imply that young children in particular are mere passive recipients of a culturally transmitted corpus of knowledge and understandings. In the extract that follows Colwyn Trevarthen eloquently explores what he describes elsewhere in the same article as the 'innate need that children have to live and learn in culture, as fish swim in the sea and birds fly in the air'. As you read the extract think about the extent to which knowledge is being described as something that is a co-construction between individuals and how this interaction with other individuals is also seen as a co-construction with a broader culture.

EXTRACT FIVE

Trevarthen, C. (1998) The child's need to learn a culture, in Woodhead, M., Faulkner, D. and Uttleton, K. (eds) Cultural worlds of early childhood. London. Routledge/Open University, pp87–89 (originally published in journal, Children and Society, 9 (1), 1995)

Meanings, it must be said, are discovered in our community by people comparing, negotiating, persuading, showing their interests to others. We can construct together only by allowing turns in initiative. These cooperative skills have a strong innate foundation, as is made clear by the way in which very young infants become involved in 'protoconversational' exchanges of expression with other persons, and by the rapid development of enjoyment in games in which events and actions on objects are made to be part of rhythmic expressions and their use is negotiated in interactions.

Infants can learn, at least from about four months of age, to join in musical or periodic games and dance-like body play, if partners are willing to watch the infant's own forms of expressions of fun and imitation. The adult has to enjoy acting like an enhancing mirror, and be prepared to have the game played back by the baby. From the interactive rituals of these games with their teasing and jokes comes, by a remarkable internally generated change in the infant's thinking at about nine months after birth, an eagerness to perceive and act vis à vis the shared world as others do. This causes objects and actions on them to be endowed with common interest, and the baby, still far from using language, starts to notice trappings of culture, like clothes, books, toys, ways of posing and gesturing, and to use them for 'showing off' the knowledge gained.

We see nothing like this behaviour in any animal, even the socially very clever apes. One-year-old children are profiting from development of the amazing appetite for common knowing, the rudiments of which showed from birth, and from the desire that develops in them during the first year to have fun in games that involve friendly teasing. They transform their communicative interest to take an active, responsible place in the community of arbitrary meanings that the older members of the family and familiar work-a-day community take for granted.

POINTS TO CONSIDER

- *Can you think of examples of children proactively seeking interactions with others?*

- *What opportunities can you provide in your work with young children for such interactive experiences?*

- *Trevarthen mentions 'interactive rituals'. Can you think of some additional examples of these?*

- *Can an Early Years setting have its own cultural rituals and practices? What might be the implications of these for children's learning?*

- *The notion of the co-construction of meaning is something you may wish to follow up by reading the work of Rogoff (1990) and also the work of Anning et al. (2004).*

CHAPTER SUMMARY

In this chapter you have been able to read extracts from some of the classic accounts of how children learn and have had the opportunity to consider some of the similarities and differences between these. In particular, the extent to which learning is essentially an individual process (Piaget) or a more social one (Vygotsky) has been addressed. You will have noted how the contributions of various theorists and authors over time build upon one another, retaining some elements of previous thinking, e.g. the notion of a child that is active in his or her own learning but also developing a new consensus in thinking, e.g. that the process of learning may be seen as a co-construction of knowledge between individuals within particular cultural contexts. You have also seen in the extract from Donaldson how the methodology behind particular theoretical accounts is a crucial aspect to consider when evaluating their theoretical conclusions. Throughout the chapter you have been encouraged to think about how theories may link in to practice within EY settings and to strive to be a professional who is prepared to evaluate theoretical accounts in order to consolidate or maybe to develop what you do within your practice.

REFERENCES

Bredekamp, S. and Copple, C. (1997) *Developmentally appropriate practice*. Washington, DC: National Association for the Education of Young Children.

CWDC (2007) *Guidance to the standards for the award of Early Years Professional Status*. Leeds: CWDC.

David, T., Goouch, K., Powell, S. and Abbott, L. (2003) *Birth To Three Matters: A review of the literature*. Nottingham: Queen's Printer.

DfES (2007) Early Years Foundation Stage. **www.standards.dfes.gov.uk/eyfs/site/index.htm** Accessed 27.03.07.

Donaldson, M. (1987) *Children's minds*. London: Fontana Press.

Honey, P. and Mumford, A. (1992) *The manual of learning styles* (3rd edn). Maidenhead: Open University Press.

Piaget, J. (1962) *The stages of the intellectual development of the child*, re-printed in A. Slater and D. Muir (1999) *The Blackwell Reader in Developmental Psychology*. Oxford: Blackwell Publishers.

Piaget, J. and Inhelder, B. (1966) *The psychology of the child*. London: Routledge and Kegan Paul.

Penn, H. (2005) *Understanding early childhood: Issues and controversies*. Maidenhead: McGraw-Hill Education.

QCA (2000) *Curriculum Guidance for the Foundation Stage*. London: QCA.

Rogoff, B. (1990) *Apprenticeship in thinking*. Oxford: Oxford University Press.

Rogoff, B. and Morelli, G. (1989) *Perspectives on children's development from cultural psychology*, reprinted in M. Gauvain and M. Cole (eds) (1993) *Readings on the Development of Children*. New York: Scientific American Books.

Siraj-Blatchford, I., Sylva, K., Muttock, S., Gilden, R. and Bell, D. (2002) *Researching effective pedagogy in the early years*. London: DfES/Crown Copyright.

Skinner, B.F. (1974) *About behaviourism*. London: Jonathan Cape.

Sylva, K., Melhuish, E., Sammons, P., Siraj-Blatchford, I. and Taggart, B. (2004) *The effective provision of pre-school education: Final report*. Nottingham: DfES Publications.

Trevarthen, C. (1998) The child's need to learn a culture, in M. Woodhead, D. Faulkner and K. Littleton, (eds) *Cultural worlds of early childhood*. London: Routledge/Open University, pp. 87–9 (originally published in *Children and Society*, 9 (1), (1995).

Vygotsky L. S. (1978) Mind in society. *The development of higher psychological processes*. Cambridge, MA: Harvard University Press.

Wood, D., Bruner, J. and Ross, G. (1976) The role of tutoring in problem solving, *Journal of Child Psychology and Psychiatry and Allied Disciplines*, 17 (2), 89–100.

FURTHER READING

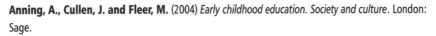

Anning, A., Cullen, J. and Fleer, M. (2004) *Early childhood education. Society and culture*. London: Sage.

Bredekamp, S. and Copple, C. (1997) *Developmentally appropriate practice*. Washington, DC: National Association for the Education of Young Children.

Sylva, K., Melhuish, E., Sammons, P., Siraj-Blatchford, I. and Taggart, B. (2004) *The Effective provision of pre-school education: Final report*. Nottingham: DfES Publications.

Chapter 4
Developing as a strong and healthy child?

Carolyn Silberfeld

This chapter will consider, in greater depth, some of the key issues which influence the health of children and how they, in turn, influence professionalism and practice.

O B J E C T I V E S

By the end of this chapter you should have:
- re-examined the issues which underpin child health and child health policy;
- evaluated the process and effectiveness of child health screening;
- evaluated the effectiveness of health promotion;
- re-explored the concept of working with families and communities;
- explored the implications of having a child with a disability/chronic health condition and the ways in which practitioners work in partnership with parents.

Professional Standards for EYPS: S3, S5, S6, S10, S18, S19, S20, S23, S30, S31, S32.

Introduction

The notions of a 'strong child' and a 'healthy child' are taken from the Birth to Three Matters Framework (DfES, 2002), guidance written for Early Years practitioners, which attempted to look at children in a holistic way while offering the practitioner time to reflect on their practice with young children. However, this concept of a strong and healthy child is rather strange and prompts me to ask several questions about its meaning and significance. If children are not strong and healthy, are they weak and unhealthy? How are strength and health defined? How can strength and health be measured? Do all children have the opportunity to be strong and healthy? Is the notion of the strong and healthy child yet another rhetorical phrase that sounds good but is not attainable or measurable for all children?

Despite greater knowledge and understanding about health promotion and disease eradication, the health of children continues to cause global concern. Within the UK, during the past ten years, there has been increased prosperity with a reduction in infant mortality from 6 to 5 per 1,000 live births, and under-5 mortality from 7 to 6 per 1,000 live births

(UNICEF, 1996, UNICEF, 2006), yet the gap between rich and poor continues to widen. The UK is now considered, by the United Nations Development Programme, to be one of the most unequal industrialised nations in the world in relation to child health. The infant mortality rate for those who are poor is 70 per cent greater than for those who are in the highest income bracket and children in low socioeconomic groups are four times more likely to die from an accident. This inequality in health outcome has been reflected in the inequality of access to health care for young children and their families. For example, the proportion of children accessing child health surveillance programmes differs widely, with more than 80 per cent being seen in more prosperous geographical areas in contrast to less than 50 per cent of children who live in poor areas (Hall and Elliman, 2006).

As signatories to the UN Convention on the Rights of the Child, recent UK government policies have attempted to redress many of these inequities whilst promoting the right of all children to have access to good quality health care and protection (DfES, 2006; DoH, 2004b). Within these policies, poverty, deprivation and inequality are recognised as being determinants of poor health and there is recognition of the need to support children and families, particularly those most vulnerable. The sentiments seem sincere and are championed by most health professionals and practitioners, including those who work with young children and their families. However, at the same time, there is a continued move to decentralise health services into local health trusts, which may have already experienced several reorganisations, who are desperately trying to reach targets of health provision set nationally, while having to rationalise the care they offer because of budgets that are unable to cope with the spiralling costs of this provision. Setting targets may be seen to be an incentive for those concerned with the health of young children and their families, but it also puts in place a mechanism to penalise those services that do not achieve their targets. Setting targets also implies individual responsibility, rather than the collective responsibility that is behind the message that health should be for all children, regardless of whether they are rich or poor. Therefore the concept of a 'strong and healthy child' needs to be questioned and challenged by those who are implementing the new Early Years Foundation Stage (EYFS) (DfES, 2007), the latest statutory framework which is based on standards which professionals and practitioners should strive to identify and promote.

In marked contrast to the contemporary concept of the child as an individual and an understanding that child health and development in children cannot be predestined, the new EYFS offers guidance about child health and development which is firmly rooted in an age-stage framework, which, however comprehensive, remains de-contextualised. This does not encourage the professional or practitioner to look at the child in its cultural, social, political and economic context. Instead, the reality may be that for most practitioners trying to fulfil all the new requirements in a limited time with limited resources, observations are limited to what is on the checklist of requirements. As well as possibly missing important information about the child, health and development are normalised in a particular, rather static way, which does not allow for individual differences and does not really value the findings from cross-cultural analyses of childhood (James and Prout, 1990) about the variety of ways in which childhood is experienced. The health of children cannot be predetermined by these standards or checklists, particularly when health provision and access to health services remains so inequitable for young children and their families.

The three extracts in this chapter challenge you to critically analyse and evaluate the implications of the broader and wider perspectives of issues in child health, in order to better understand your role as a professional and practitioner who works with young children and their families.

Panter-Brick, C. (ed.) (1998) **Biosocial perspectives on children.** *Cambridge: Cambridge University Press, pp67–70*

Measuring outcomes of ill-health

For the tools of their trade, biological anthropologists have developed a number of trusted indicators of child health and ill-health. Two of the most important indicators are demographic and anthropometric parameters (Table 4.1). Because the literature on health issues is so extensive (Hansluwka, 1985), I wish here only to highlight useful means of presenting relevant data and some of the controversies regarding their interpretation.

It is worth spelling out the reasons why both demographic and anthropometric indicators have been widely used in cross-cultural studies of child health. First of all, these kinds of data are relatively easy to obtain – namely, information on births, deaths, heights and weights. Second, there exists a large comparative body of data for Western and non-Western populations (derived from censuses, world fertility surveys, national and community-based growth studies) available for comparative purposes. Third, both mortality and growth rates among children are considered to be sensitive to poor environmental conditions (Harrison et al., 1990; Mascie-Taylor, 1991). Thus, in developing countries like The Gambia, the 'growth rate is very clearly related to climatic factors associated with the timing of the rainy season or seasons, through their influence on food availability, parasite load . . . and infection' (Cole, 1993: 89). Childhood mortality rates have also been shown to vary seasonally in many developing countries, for example in Nepal and The Gambia (Nabarro, 1984; Ulijaszek, 1993).

Table 4.1. *Indicators of child health: integrating measures on the outcomes of ill-health with information on social and ecological contexts*

Macro-level data on outcomes	Contextual data
Demographic indicators	
Fertility	Weaning, childcare practices
Mortality	Birth intervals
Morbidity	Poverty, education
Anthropometric indicators	
Weight, height	Malnutrition
Height-for-age (stunting)	Infection
Weight-for-height (wasting)	Household composition
Weight-for-age (underweight)	

Demographic indicators

Demographers have subdivided childhood into different time intervals to better examine the rates and causes of child deaths. Thus, infant mortality refers to the number of deaths under 1 year of age (per 1,000 live births), while child mortality is usually taken as the number of deaths from age 1 year to 5 years. Low infant and child mortality rates are sensitive measures of community well-being, and thus of the adequacy of public health (Allen and Thomas, 1992; Tilford, 1995; UNICEF, 1996).

In Western countries, the greatest improvements in mortality have taken place for postneonatal infant mortality through public health measures and medical care. The causes of postneonatal mortality (I–12 months of age) are mostly infections and accidents, whereas neonatal mortality (in the first month of life) is due to birth injuries, prematurity or malformations. An example will illustrate the dramatic decrease in infant deaths. In 1662, John Gaunt recorded an infant mortality in Great Britain of the order of 300 deaths per 1000 live births; by 1901, this rate was only 151 deaths, and by 1985, only 9.4 deaths per 1000 live births (Pollard et al., 1974; 68).

Developing countries can be ranked according to their infant and child mortality rates in order to draw attention to problems of poverty and ill-health. Using data from the 1976 World Fertility Survey, Hobcraft et al. (1984) showed that Senegal, Nepal and Bangladesh had the highest overall mortality rates for under-fives among 28 Third World countries (Table 4.2). Nepal and Bangladesh had the highest infant mortality (accounting for two-thirds of total deaths), while Senegal had the highest child mortality (half the deaths occurred at ages 1 to 5 years). This picture helped to pin-point periods of childhood vulnerability, associated with extreme poverty in all three countries, and specifically in Senegal with the weaning period, after the first year of life.

Hobcraft et al. (1983) also used the World Fertility Survey to show that closely spaced births have a negative impact on mortality rates, of both the index child and subsequent children. Where birth intervals were short (less than 2 years apart), the index child showed a greater risk of mortality in nine of the 23 countries studied; this could be explained by premature weaning if the mother was newly pregnant. The subsequent child also showed an elevated risk of death (by 50%) in 13 of the countries surveyed. Two hypotheses are commonly offered to explain why short birth intervals elevate the mortality of subsequent children: a maternal depletion syndrome (whereby a mother may start her reproductive life underweight, sustains repeated pregnancies and lactation, and gives birth to a small baby, which has poorer chances of survival), and sibling competition (for scarce household resources or maternal attention). Thus, demographers have shown that birth interval, along with mother's education (Cleland and van Ginneken, 1988), emerges as one of the most significant factors to influence variation in mortality rates for children under 5 years of age (Hobcraft et al., 1985).

EXTRACT ONE continued

Table 4.2. *Use of demographic indicators. National mortality rates for children in the first 5 years of life*

	Infant 0-1 year /1000(%)	Child 1-5 years /1000(%)	Under-fives 0-5 years /1000 (%)
Senegal	123[6] (43)	164[1] (57)	287[1] (100)
Nepal	166[1] (64)	93[2] (36)	259[2] (100)
Bangladesh	141[2] (66)	74[3] (34)	215[3] (100)

Notes:
Superscripts are rankings among 28 Third World countries.
Source: *Data from Hobcraft et al. (1984). World Fertility Survey (1976).*

Anthropologists have also used these indicators to characterise the health conse-quences of childcare behaviours at community or household level. For instance, Hewlett (1991) reviewed the extent to which demographic parameters (total fertility, infant and child mortality, age and sex composition) explained cross-cultural varia-tion in childcare practices (such as single versus multiple caregiving, male-biased sex ratios and step-parenting) among hunter/gatherers, horticulturalists and pastoralists. This type of analysis provides a useful socioecological context to data on mortality rates, which are otherwise used at a global level as indicators of community health (Newell and Nabarro, 1989) (Table 4.1).

It is very difficult to measure health and well-being, so measurements relating to the level of disease and death are usually an indication of whether or not an individual, population or community are healthy. Instead of looking at world patterns of health we are forced to look at world patterns of disease and disability and in doing so, it is necessary to use well-defined and perhaps rather rigid and limited definitions of disease and disability.

In this extract the reader is introduced to one of the ways in which child health can be measured. Similar to other ways of calculating how healthy a population is, level of ill-health, such as mortality and morbidity, are the units of measurement. Whilst these measurements suggest that levels of ill-health are linked to geographic and environmental factors, it is clear that the least healthy children live in poor countries and that those who have access to health care have a better chance of survival and well-being.

The UK is considered to be a wealthy country with universal access to health provision and health care based on the need of the individual, rather than the ability to pay. The National Health Service has undergone several major reforms since its inception in 1948, one of the most recent being an emphasis on giving patients more choice in what, where and how they receive the care that they require. In order to achieve this, further restructuring has taken place and the NHS now has new partners which include social care providers, the independent sector, and the voluntary and community sector. Additionally standards and targets have been set for Health Trusts, the achievement of which is linked to levels of funding (DoH, 2004a; DoH, 2006). With the Every Child Matters agenda (DfES, 2003) and its sequel *Every Child Matters: Next Steps* (DfES, 2004), child health and welfare have also become prioritised in new policy directives relating to child protection (DfES, 2006) and services for children (DoH, 2004b). Once again, standards for protection and care and service provision have been delineated and have now become part of statutory responsibility. Although the child protection policy referred to in the previous sentence has been newly updated (DfES, 2006), it has developed from an earlier version published in 1999.

POINTS TO CONSIDER

With such comprehensive child health policy in place, supposedly for all children, you need to begin to reflect on the following questions.

- *Why is the infant mortality rate for those who are poor 70 per cent greater than for those who are in the highest income bracket?*

- *Why are children in low socioeconomic groups four times more likely to die from an accident?*

Panter-Brick (1998) suggests that contextualising global demographic and anthropometric indicators, by linking them to socio-ecological factors, is useful because this provides contextual meaning to such measurements as mortality and morbidity which are used to indicate levels of child survival, health and well-being. However, even this only really offers a superficial understanding of children's health and well-being. Such outcome measures do not allow for interrogation of the processes involved in the way children survive and cope with difficult physical, emotional and environmental difficulties.

There is also the question of whether global and anthropometric indicators can be applied cross-culturally. Later on in the chapter, Panter-Brick (1998, p94) acknowledges that there are 'critical differences in parental appreciation of child health and malnutrition'. By this she is referring to the different ways in which child health needs are prioritised. Using a thought-provoking example, Panter-Brick (1998, p94) questions whether the Western approach to child survival – saving life at all costs – can be seen as 'misguided' if issues relating to poverty and inequality are not addressed at the same time.

Panter-Brick (1998) also offers the example of the way in which food, where it is scarce, is allocated in households where economic contribution is prioritised, rather than the nutritional needs of the individual. This is in contrast to the emphasis, in the UK, on the need to meet the nutritional needs of the child in order to help them develop into healthy adults. Whilst one approach might be perceived as a short-term strategy and the other as a long-term strategy, both strategies are responding to the particular context in which they are employed, so neither can be seen as more appropriate than the other.

Improving the nutritional status of children and reducing the levels of childhood obesity are high on the UK policy agenda.

Health promotion initiatives can offer information, guidance and, to a certain extent, support for children and families whose nutritional status is compromised. It has been suggested that providing healthy food for children need not be expensive. However, this assumes that parents have access to appropriate cooking facilities and the time to shop, prepare and cook nutritionally balanced meals. Time poverty is a factor in both economically rich and economically poor families. Although parents' own dietary habits have been found to influence the nutritional intake of their children (Longbottom *et al.*, 2002), more powerful influences on the healthiness of a child's diet are linked to limited income, local availability of fresh foods, transport issues affecting accessibility, lack of opportunities to learn cooking skills, and children's experiences of food outside the home (White, 2003). Although parents understand healthy-food messages, food choices are restricted by financial considerations. It is somewhat of a 'Catch 22' situation – a limited income does not allow for any wastage of food that children do not like, and their ensuing hunger. Health belief and health behaviour are often in conflict with each other. As a result parents on a limited income may be compromised into buying food that they know their children will eat, rather than the food they know to be healthier (Price, 2007).

In an effort to provide nutritional support for low-income families, the Department of Health has decided to replace the milk-only Welfare Food Scheme with a new initiative called Healthy Start (DoH, 2004c). With the aim of tackling rising levels of obesity in children under four years old, families claiming financial support for their income receive weekly vouchers to spend on milk, fruit and vegetables. Although in principle this seems a commendable initiative, there are growing concerns that rates of iron-deficiency anaemia, which are still more prevalent among young children than obesity, may increase still further (More, 2004). Of concern is that infant formula will no longer be sold at reduced prices in health clinics and health centres and parents may use the vouchers for cow's milk, which is cheaper than formula milk.

POINTS TO CONSIDER

Using your knowledge and understanding about nutrition in children reflect on the following:

- *How can you, as a professional or practitioner working with children, influence the nutritional practice of young children and their families? Consider the effectiveness of the strategy you have outlined.*

EXTRACT TWO

British Medical Association (1999) Growing up in Britain: Ensuring a healthy future for our children. *London: BMJ Books, pp17–19 and 29–30*

Key health issues for children today

The major demographic, social, behavioural and medical developments which have occurred over this century have been reflected in the changes which have occurred in the health of the childhood population.[9] The most significant change in child health has been the rapid fall in deaths and morbidity from acute infections such as tuberculosis, measles, and whooping cough, which can be attributed to improvements in hygiene, living conditions, antibiotics, and immunisation. However, there is emerging evidence that the quality of children's health is being threatened by new problems of different types which relate to the effects of adverse demographic, economic and cultural developments;[9] for example, the increased prevalence of mental and emotional problems, asthma, and obesity. The World Health Organisation has projected that in the next 30 years, injury will overtake infectious disease as the major reason for global loss of healthy life years.[10]

Infant mortality

The Chief Medical Officer for England and Wales in his annual statement 'On the State of the Public Health 1997' reported that the infant mortality rate had fallen to the lowest ever recorded with 5.9 babies dying per 1000 live births (Figure 2.4). In 1996, 3725 babies died before the age of 1 year, this fell to 3591 in 1997. During 1996 in England, there were 3345 stillbirths compared to 3250 in 1997. The stillbirth rate fell from 5.5 to 5.4 per 1000 total births between 1995 and 1996.[11] Worldwide, the infant mortality rate was 59 per 1000 live births in 1995.[10]

There has also been a large fall in recent years of postneonatal deaths, from 4.1 per 1000 live births in 1988 to 3.0 per 1000 in 1991. This has been almost entirely attributed to a fall in deaths from Sudden Infant Death Syndrome (SIDS).[9] In 1982, the mortality rate attributed to SIDS was 1.73 per 1000 live births, this declined to 1.25 in l991.[9] SIDS, however, is still the largest single cause of infant death in the postneonatal period, accounting for 30% of all postneonatal deaths in England and Wales in 1992.[9]

Childhood mortality

Childhood mortality rates are at an historically low level and Figure 2.5 illustrates the main causes of childhood mortality by age and sex in England and Wales in 1991.

Injury and poisoning is the single commonest cause of death for boys of all ages outside infancy and for girls aged 5 and over. In 1991, cancer was the cause of 13% of deaths among children aged 1–4, although mortality from cancer has decreased over recent years. Congenital malformations account for almost one in five deaths under the age of 5. In 1971, child deaths due to diseases of the respiratory system were still a significant cause of mortality, accounting for 16.5% of child deaths; however, in 1991, this had declined to 8.5%.[9] Infectious diseases are much less likely to cause death and serious illness than at the turn of the century. In 1981, 15 children died of measles, in 1991, only one (Figure 2.6).[9]

Trends in childhood morbidity

Over the past 20 years, there has been little change in the incidence of childhood cancers but between 1970 and 1985, hospital admissions for child cancer patients increased more than fourfold. However mortality rates have decreased slightly, which leads to the conclusion that improvements in treatment mean that children now survive for longer and many are cured.[9] The most common types of child cancer are leukaemia and brain tumours.

Definitions of disadvantage

There are difficulties with the measures used to categorise individuals into groups that relate to their level of deprivation.[6] Social class is a widely used measure, however this is not necessarily an indicator of 'material' wealth that is, housing, adequate income, etc. Material disadvantage may be absolute, relative, or both. Children and other family members are classified according to the occupation of the main earner in the family. Occupation is therefore used as a proxy measure of income. Social class is perhaps becoming a poorer measure of socio-economic status than in the past, as home ownership, second incomes, single parenthood and unemployment cut across the traditional relationship between husband's occupation and family resources. Using class-based analysis excludes people classified as unoccupied, for example, economically inactive single mothers.[7] This group are a high risk group for living in poverty as well as experiencing relatively high risks of child mortality. The longitudinal studies of the Office of Population Censuses and Surveys (OPCS)[8] have demonstrated the value of other measures of social and economic circumstances, such as housing tenure and car ownership. These have been found to be more effective discriminators of mortality differences than social class and do not exclude economically inactive people.

For children it is not solely material wealth that matters and their well-being is directly related to their emotional environment. However materially privileged a child's family is, problems will arise if they are unwanted or resented, neglected or abused. Poverty, unemployment or homelessness may exert their effect on the child by the overall reduction in parental capacity to meet their own and their children's emotional needs. With regard to children, social disadvantage is therefore probably best considered in terms of the quality of child care. Good child care involves a mutually affectionate relationship based on respect, empathy and genuineness with one or preferably more adults, consistent discipline based on positive reward for good behaviour rather than punishment for bad, and intellectual stimulation appropriate to the child's level of development.

Socio-economic inequalities and health

The OPCS report The Health of Our Children[9] *and the Office for National Statistics (ONS) report* Health Inequalities[10] *have reviewed data for childhood mortality and morbidity and have drawn a number of key points from the data.*

- *During the 1980s and early 1990s infant and childhood mortality rates fell for all social classes, but the social class differentials persisted. In 1993–95 the infant mortality rate for social class V births was 70% higher than that of social class I births.*

- *Babies born weighing under 2500 g in 1991 accounted for 59% of neonatal deaths. In 1994 in England and Wales the average birthweight in social class V was 115 g lighter than in social class I for births inside marriage and 130 g lighter for births outside marriage registered by both parents.*

- *In 1993 the Children's Dental Health. Survey found that among 12 year olds 45% from non-manual households suffered from any form of decay, compared to 68% from unskilled manual households.*

- *Childhood mortality from injury and poisoning fell between the early 1980s and early 1990s for all social classes. However the differential between the classes increased as a result of the smaller decline occurring in social classes IV and V as compared to social classes I and II.*

Continuing with a theme of measuring health, the first part of this extract outlines the trends in childhood mortality from 1971 to 1991, noting the steady decrease in the overall measurement. Although the causes of mortality remain similar, the incidence of these causes has changed. Death from infection and respiratory illness has declined, whereas mortality associated with accidents and poisonings has increased to become the most common cause of death in young children. Perhaps surprisingly, there has not been much difference in the incidence of death due to childhood cancers, nor from congenital abnormalities.

Of note, too, is the difference between the causes of infant mortality and under-5 mortality in both girls and boys. Whereas sudden infant death syndrome accounted for 41 per cent mortality in infants, it accounted for only 4 per cent mortality in children aged between 1 and 5 years old. In contrast, injury and poisoning accounted for 22 per cent mortality compared to 5 per cent mortality in infants. Both groups have similar mortality rates for deaths associated with respiratory disease and congenital abnormalities.

Between 1990 and 1996 there was a steady but sharp increase (700 per cent) in the number of children who died from AIDS and AIDS-related illness, mainly from 'mother to child transmission'. Since 1997 mortality related to AIDS has declined markedly, thought mainly to be due to the intervention with antiretroviral treatment, improved management of opportunistic infections and the avoidance of breastfeeding, but is still seen as an important cause of child mortality (Gibb, 2003).

POINTS TO CONSIDER

- *Why have the causes of mortality in children changed during the past 30 years?*
- *Why is AIDS thought to be an important cause of child mortality, despite the reduction in incidence since 1997?*

Childhood morbidity is an indication of the illness and disability arising from diseases or conditions. However, it is extremely difficult to measure morbidity because definitions of illness are, to some extent, subjective and illnesses can vary greatly in severity and duration. Morbidity rates in children tend to be linked to hospital admissions, visits to the GP and days absent from school. In an observational study of 93,356 children aged between 0 and 15 years of age, differences in morbidity in children in households with one adult presenting to general practitioners were compared with children in households with more than one adult (Fleming and Charlton, 1998).

Not surprisingly, children in households with one adult were found to consult general practitioners more frequently than those in households with two or more adults, received increased numbers of home visits, were more likely to consult for accidents, and attended less frequently for immunisation. The discussion of these results linked the findings to levels of deprivation and poverty, and the additional burdens for general practitioners. Recommendations focused on the need for more specific targeting by general practitioners, health visitors, and primary healthcare workers for accident prevention and immunisation uptake, yet there was little discussion regarding some of the more logical explanations for the findings.

One of the fastest-growing conditions in young children is mental ill-health. Some of the statistics that have been put forward by the Mental Health Foundation make worrying reading. They estimate that one in five children suffer from mental health problems which include anxiety disorders, eating disorders and depression. Mental health problems have an identifiable link with poverty, inequality and deprivation. Other contributory factors are thought to be related to modern lifestyles, in which there is an emphasis on material rewards and physical safety. Growing concerns by parents about letting children play outside and more regimented approaches to outdoor play in some Early Years settings (health and safety) mean that children may be deprived of activities which develop skills and abilities which cannot be covered by curricula. New curricula guidelines and constraints are also thought to be reducing the time and space for children to develop their imaginative and creative skills and abilities.

In the second part of the BMA (1999) extract there is a reiteration of the statement that despite the improvement of the health of children in the UK, geographical, social class and ethnic variations persist, and that the health inequalities between rich and poor are becoming even wider. There is the recognition that although childhood mortality rates are declining, there is an increase in the rates of childhood morbidity. There is also consideration of the social and economic determinants of health, such as poor housing, unemployment and poverty, which were identified nearly 20 years ago in the Black Report (1980) and the effects that these can have on maternal and child health.

In an attempt to define disadvantage there is an acknowledgement that it is extremely difficult to measure levels of deprivation and that high levels of unemployment have meant that previous ways of measuring socioeconomic status, through the occupation of the main earner in a family, can no longer be used. The term 'disadvantage' can also be applied to children, whose emotional and psychological needs are not being met, even when they are financially secure.

In 2001 a groundbreaking report into the state of London's children (Hood, 2001) showed that even in Europe's richest city, children were caught up in a spiral of poverty and exclusion. The report portrayed an overwhelming picture of the way in which poverty and social exclusion had created a divided city in which the most vulnerable children were the main casualties. It found that 43 per cent of London children lived in poverty – more than any other English Region – and that this even rose to 74 per cent in one borough.

London schools permanently excluded more children than the national average, large numbers of whom were black or had special educational needs, and it was found that children in inner London were less likely to achieve at school.

More babies died in London, and the city had more chronically ill children than the national average. Children living in poverty were five times more likely to die from accidents and three times more likely to have mental ill-health than children in homes with average income. In London, facilities, amenities and attractions were beyond financial reach of many poor children. As well as having less access to public or private transport, they were also more likely to live in overcrowded and poor-quality housing.

Children were consulted about their views on living in London. The responses identified clear ways in which children could have a better quality of life and be better protected. The report recommended more co-ordinated policymaking, the need to respect every child's right to be part of decision-making and that unless child poverty was adequately addressed any meaningful change would be difficult to achieve.

POINTS TO CONSIDER

- *With reference to the key points drawn from the data on socioeconomic inequalities and child health on page 57, how could these inequalities be reduced?*

- *Using your own experience, how can Early Years professionals and practitioners help others to understand the complexities of socioeconomic inequalities and the effects on child health?*

EXTRACT THREE

Hall, D. and Elliman, D. (2006) **Health for all children** *(rev 4th ed.). Oxford: Oxford University Press, pp132–134*

The role of formal screening programmes

Some defects are unlikely to be recognized even by the most astute parent and can only be detected by health professionals if a specific search is made. Examples include dislocation of the hip before the child starts to walk, high-frequency hearing loss prior to the age when speech normally begins, some congenital heart defects, and congenital cataracts. The detection of such defects might be achieved by the use of specific screening tests. This is discussed below.

The need for professional sensitivity

When a problem has been overlooked by parents, its identification by professionals in the course of screening or routine reviews is often welcomed. There may also be less positive responses, though these may be concealed. Parents may have been actively denying the possibility of there being anything wrong with the child to protect themselves or their partners against a distressing experience; this may happen particularly at times when they are having to deal with several other sources of stress and anxiety. Alternatively, parents may feel guilt that they had failed to identify the problem or act upon it until it was pointed out to them. As some disorders have a genetic component, this can add to feelings of guilt.

These phenomena are not a reason for withholding information or failing to be honest about one's suspicions, but they do highlight the need for professional skill, sensitivity, and follow-up support and guidance when seeing children.

Screening

Definition

Screening was defined by the American Commission on Chronic Illness in 1957 as 'the presumptive identification of unrecognized disease or defect by the application

EXTRACT THREE *continued*

of tests, examinations and other procedures, which can be applied rapidly. Screening tests sort out apparently well persons who may have a disease from those who probably do not. A screening test is not intended to be diagnostic'.

In essence a screening procedure (which may be a test or questionnaire) is applied to a population who have no manifestations of a disorder to separate out those at higher risk from those at lower risk. The former then proceed to have a definitive diagnostic test. No screening test is 100 per cent perfect in that 'cases' are missed ('false negative'), people without the disorder are falsely labelled as having it ('false positive'), and some may be harmed by the procedure.

Criteria for screening programmes and tests

The concept of screening is attractive. It makes good sense to identify disease or disorder at a pre-symptomatic stage in order to correct it before too much damage is done. Recognizing that the number of diseases for which screening might in theory be possible is almost unlimited, Wilson and Yungner devised a set of criteria by which screening programmes could be evaluated (Table 6.1). These have been modified by the UK National Screening Committee (NSC).

Table 6.1 *Wilson and Jungner's criteria for screening programmes*

---

1 The condition to be sought should be an important public health problem *as judged by the potential for health achievable by early diagnosis.*

2 There should be an accepted treatment *or other beneficial intervention for* patients with recognized *or occult* disease.

3 Facilities for diagnosis and treatment should be available *and shown to be working effectively for classic cares of the condition in question.*

4 There should be a latent or early symptomatic stage *and the extent to which this can be recognized by parents and professionals should be known.*

5 There should be a suitable test or examination: it should be simple, valid for the condition in question, reasonably priced, repeatable in different trials or circumstances, sensitive and specific: the test should be acceptable to *the majority* of the population.

6 The natural history of the condition *and of conditions which may mimic it* should be understood.

7 There should be an agreed definition of what is meant by a case of the target disorder, and *also an agreement as to (i) which other conditions are likely to be detected by the screening programme and (ii) whether their detection will be an advantage or a disadvantage.*

8 Treatment at the early, latent, or presymptomatic phase should favourably influence prognosis, *or improve outcome for the family as a whole.*

9 The cost of screening should be economically balanced in relation to expenditure on the care and treatment of persons with the disorder and to medical care as a whole.

10 Case finding *may need to be* a continuous process and not a once and for all project, *but there should be explicit justification for repeated screening procedures or stages*

Modifications proposed to increase relevance for paediatric practice are shown in italics.

▶

Cochrane and Holland described the characteristics of the ideal screening test as follows.

1 *Simple, quick and easy to interpret; capable of being performed by paramedics or other personnel.*

2 *Acceptable to the public, since participation in screening programmes is voluntary.*

3 *Accurate, i.e. gives a true measurement of the attribute under investigation.*

4 *Repeatable: this involves the components of observer variability (both within and between tests), subject variability, and test variability.*

5 *Sensitive: this is the ability of a test to give a positive finding when the individual screened has the disease or abnormality under investigation.*

6 *Specific: this is the ability of the test to give a negative finding when the individual does not have the disease or abnormality under investigation.*

Rose added the concept of 'yield' which was defined as the number of new previously unsuspected cases detected per 100 individuals screened. Haggard pointed out that the yield of a screening test declines as case-finding by other means becomes increasingly effective . . . and coined the term 'incremental yield'.

Formal and opportunistic screening

Formal screening programmes aimed at the whole population are one of the means by which early detection is accomplished, but are not the only method nor necessarily the most important. Opportunistic screening is similar to formal screening except that the initial contact is initiated by the parents for some other purpose and the professional uses the contact to carry out one or more screening tests or procedures. In contrast with formal screening programmes, opportunistic screening does not incorporate the requirement to seek out all the children in the population so that they can be screened. However, the health professional still has a responsibility to ensure that the procedure satisfies the basic criteria for a screening test.

The final extract introduces you to the role of formal and opportunistic child health surveillance programmes and the criteria that should be applied for any screening or test carried out on young children. Although there is now a much greater emphasis on the need for prevention in child health promotion programmes, rather than the detection of disorders, screening is still thought to be of use within a more holistic approach to promoting the health of children. This new approach to health promotion has moved away from the traditional one-to-one interventions which traditionally offered information and advice, to one of a community-based approach, which recognises that relationships and community-wide issues, such as housing and safety, need to be addressed if health promotion is to be effective. Health promotion is seen much more as a collective, rather than individualistic, approach, which, by valuing the contributions of families and communities, can improve health outcomes for everyone. Valuing the contributions of families and communities implies more than just rhetoric – it involves mutually trusting relationships in which everyone involved is regarded with esteem and included within any planning or process.

- *How can child health and well-being be promoted in Early Years settings, using such a holistic approach?*

The extract offers a somewhat cumbersome medical definition of screening. Perhaps a more reader-friendly definition is that offered by Bedford *et al.* (2004, p7), in which screening is defined as being 'to identify a group in the population who are at higher risk of a specific condition and who would benefit from further investigation to determine if they would profit from some form of intervention'. Earlier in the text from which this extract has been taken, Hall and Elliman (2006) questioned the value of screening and early detection, particularly when screening programmes have not carried out a benefit analysis or evaluation before implementing the surveillance programme. They came to the conclusion that early detection is still valuable because of the potential improved outcome of the disorder and the improved quality of life for the child and family.

The extract outlines different criteria for screening programmes and highlights the need for professional sensitivity. All screening programmes should have been approved by the National Screening Committee (NSC) set up in 1996, which has assessed them against specific criteria. It is important to remember that screening is, in general, performed on children whose parents do not suspect they have a problem. Bedford *et al.* (2004, p7) remind us that although screening can be beneficial it can also be harmful 'if poorly implemented or not well-thought out'. Parents need to be advised that screening does not always identify everyone with a particular condition. There is the recommendation, in the extract, that there should be adequate services to deliver appropriate management of any condition diagnosed as a result of screening. Interestingly, however, later on in the text Hall and Elliman (2006) propose that some screening be selective, that rather than blanket screening (apart from routine antenatal screening), the focus should be on those children, and their families who are more vulnerable in society, e.g. family history of genetic disorders, which may be perceived as a way of rationalising the cost of such programmes. Although this may prevent unnecessary screening of children, it may also be a pragmatic way of allocating limited resources.

However, there may be wider implications of such an approach. Approximately 5 per cent of infants are born with a genetic disorder and although genetic disorders are individually rare they form a large burden of mortality and morbidity.

Genetic disorders account for 50 per cent of all cases of childhood blindness and deafness, 30 per cent of all childhood admissions to hospital, and between 40 to 50 per cent of childhood deaths are due to genetic disorders or congenital abnormalities. Not least of all, genetic disorders account for approximately 40 per cent of all cases of severe developmental delay. Therefore the cost of doing selective screening only could be far greater in the long term.

Another rationalisation proposed by Hall and Elliman (2006) is a reduction in the routine screening of vision, hearing and growth in children in some parts of the UK. Their rationale is based on the lack of evidence of the benefits of routine screening, and the notion that by reducing routine surveillance for children whose parents are well able to access help when they are worried, there will be additional resources to find and review the children in most need. They acknowledge the important part played in this process by health visitors whom they consider very capable of making the decisions about who should or should not receive screening and surveillance. However, this proposal has been challenged vociferously by health professionals (Fry, 2003) as being a recipe for disaster and there is the suggestion that 'if the baby is thrown out with the bathwater, it will be a very expensive bath'. As the routine screening of children at regular intervals in childhood has been reduced over the years, Fry (2003) suggests that current pre-school and school entry screening is even more important for detecting any health deficit.

There is unanimous agreement that surveillance needs to be vigorously done by knowledgeable professionals who have received appropriate training, and are able to work sensitively with children, families and communities. Hall and Elliman (2006) suggest that all children should have a visual assessment by an orthoptist between the ages of 4 and 5 years but there are insufficient qualified orthoptists to carry this out in the foreseeable future. Neonatal hearing tests may become the only routine screening for hearing problems, and however successful they are at picking up congenital hearing disorders, this strategy will not help identify hearing conditions that develop in childhood. Traditionally routine screening has been carried out by health visitors and school nurses but both are a 'dying breed' because of Health Trust priorities (often curative health strategies at the expense of preventative health care and training for community health professionals) and an increasing number of health visitors and school nurses who are approaching retirement.

POINTS TO CONSIDER

- *What are the implications of reduced screening in children and the potential reduction in the community health professionals who perform screening and surveillance?*

Supporting children and families where screening has identified a disability or chronic condition requires specialised knowledge and understanding about the wider effects of the diagnosis on the child and family. The needs of children who have chronic illnesses, which include metabolic (e.g. cystic fibrosis), respiratory and cancerous conditions are often focused on the medical aspects of the care, which may overshadow their social, emotional, cultural and economic needs. Parents are expected to cope with the unexpected long-term changes in their lives with minimal financial emotional and social support. Although counselling may be offered, this is usually on a short-term basis and is often related to the medical condition rather than to the needs of the child and family.

Autistic spectrum disorders have become increasingly identified in young children and there is good evidence to suggest that early diagnosis of such conditions contributes to better long-term outcomes for pre-school children. A recent study which explored health visitors' perceptions of their role with families where children are diagnosed as having an autistic spectrum disorder suggested that early intervention not only minimised challenging behaviours, but also maximised developmental progress and improved parent–child relationships (Halpin and Nugent, 2007). However, there are no recommendations for routine screening for autistic spectrum disorders and the inconsistencies and delays in referral across the UK tend to impede early diagnosis. Once again, these inequalities in cash-strapped health trusts, which are trying to rationalise some of their preventative health care initiatives, have far-reaching implications for children, families and Early Years practitioners. There is an increasing need for multiprofessional working, in partnership with parents, in which there are reciprocal levels of respect for contrasting multidisciplinary perspectives and cultural practices. It is not only a question of information sharing but also the need to discuss the appropriateness of provision and support for the child and family and the reality of shared decision-making, rather than the rhetoric.

POINTS TO CONSIDER

- *What are some of the ways in which Early Years practitioners and professionals can support children who have special needs by working in partnership with parents?*

C H A P T E R   S U M M A R Y

This chapter has attempted to consider and discuss some of the key issues which influence the health of children and how these, in turn, influence professionalism and practice. Although the discussions may seem to be rather superficial, it is hoped that they have prompted you to develop and extend your knowledge and understanding about the wider issues in child health. Child health may be high on the political agenda but I would suggest that much of this prominence is more aspirational (what the government or organisations want to happen), or promotional ('selling' a new policy or strategy) rather than achievable reality. There are no easy options or solutions for addressing the poverty, deprivation and inequalities in child health and it is not the remit of this chapter to engage with the ways in which we can live in a more just and fair society. However, without an awareness of these political and economic factors it is very difficult for those who work with young children and their families to offer the necessary support required, in an attempt to ensure that Health for All Children does not become yet another unattainable goal.

Bedford, H., Elliman, D. and Hugman, J. (2004) Screening in childhood, *Community Practitioner*, 77 (1), 7–9.

Department for Education and Skills (2002) *Birth to Three Matters Framework*. Nottingham: DfES Publications.

Department for Education and Skills (2003) *Every Child Matters: Agenda for Change*. Nottingham: DfES Publications.

Department for Education and Skills (2004) *Every Child Matters: Next Steps*. Nottingham: DfES Publications.

Department for Education and Skills (2006) *Working together to safeguard children: A guide to inter-agency working to safeguard and promote the welfare of children*. Norwich: The Stationery Office.

Department for Education and Skills (2007) *Early Years Foundation Stage: Statutory Framework and Guidance*. Nottingham: DfES Publications.

Department of Health (2004a) *The NHS Improvement Plan: Putting people at the heart of public services*. Norwich: The Stationery Office.

Department of Health (2004b) *National Service Framework for Children, Young People and Maternity Services*. Norwich: The Stationery Office.

Department of Health (2004c) *Healthy Start: Government response to the consultation exercise*. London: Department of Health.

Department of Health (2006) *Our health, our care, our say: a new direction for community services*. Norwich: The Stationery Office.

Fleming, D.M. and Charlton, J.R.H. (1998) Morbidity and healthcare utilisation of children in households with one adult – a comparative observational study, *British Medical Journal*, 316, 1572–6.

Fry, T. (2003) Screening at school entry: vision, hearing and growth, *Journal of Family Health Care*, 13(4), 104–5.

Gibb, D. M. (2003) Decline in mortality, AIDS, and hospital admissions in perinatally HIV-1 infected children in the United Kingdom and Ireland, *British Medical Journal*, 327 (7422), 1019.

Hall, D. and Elliman, D. (2006) *Health for all children* (rev. 4th edn). Oxford: Oxford University Press.

Halpin, J. and Nugent, B. (2007) Health visitors' perceptions of their role in autistic spectrum disorder, *Community Practitioner*, 80 (1), 18–22.

Hood, S. (2001) *The state of London's children*. London: Office of the Children's Rights Commissioner for London.

James, A. and Prout, A. (1990) *Constructing and reconstructing childhood*. Abingdon: Falmer Press.

Longbottom, P.J., Wrieden, W.L. and Daly, L. (2002) Is there a relationship between the food intakes of Scottish $5\frac{1}{2}$–$8\frac{1}{2}$-year-olds and those of their mothers? *Journal of Human Nutrition and Dietetics*, (15), 4, 271–9.

More, J. (2004) Is Healthy Start as healthy as it could be? *Community Practitioner*, 77(7), 245–6.

Panter-Brick, C. (ed.) (1998) *Biosocial perspectives on children*. Cambridge: Cambridge University Press.

Price, L. (2007) Mothering and promoting health in a socially-deprived area, *Community Practitioner*, 80(3), 24–7.

UNICEF (1996) *The State of the World's Children 1996: 50th Anniversary Issue*. Oxford: Oxford University Press.

UNICEF (2005) *The State of the World's Children 2006: Excluded and invisible*. New York: UNICEF.

White, J. (2003) Barriers to eating 'five-a-day' fruit and vegetables, *Community Practitioner*, 76, (10), 377–80.

Chapter 5

The family and its role in development

Mary Wild

Within this chapter the role of the family in children's development will be considered.

OBJECTIVES

By the end of this chapter you should have:
- reflected on the different ways in which 'family' can be defined;
- considered the content and implications of the theory of attachment and evaluated the prominence given to the role of the mother by considering the challenge posed by the work of Rutter amongst others;
- considered relationships within the family other than parent–child relationships, focusing in particular on the relationships between siblings;
- considered the work of Bronfenbrenner, which locates the role of the family within a broader societal and cultural framework;
- thought about the implications of these different ideas for professional practice in the Early Years.

Professional Standards for EYPS: S25, S29, S30, S31, S32

As you read through the chapter you will naturally find yourself reflecting on your experiences within a family; whether from your own childhood and/or from the perspective of being a parent or grandparent yourself. If you work with young children you will also have many valuable experiences of working with potentially diverse families and may already have strong opinions about the role of the family in children's development. You will find it helpful to draw on these experiences as you reflect on the theoretical perspectives within the chapter but you may also find that your personal understandings and beliefs about the family and family life may be challenged by what you read. Acknowledging the validity of your personal perspective yet being sufficiently open-minded to embrace other ideas is a crucial balance for the professional or student within Early Years.

Introduction

'Family' is one of those evocative words that conjure up an instant mental image for most people and most probably an image that is based on your own family. It is also likely that the image you have of the family evokes strong emotional responses within you, whether positive or negative. You may look back upon your own childhood experience of the family and be certain that if you have or intend to have children you would wish to offer them a similar upbringing to your own or alternatively you may be convinced that you will definitely do things differently to your own parents. Even if you did not experience life within a family unit as a child you are likely to hold opinions about the desirability of growing up within a family and of the potential effects of family life for the development of children. Certainly, within the media and our wider cultural and political contexts, the family is commonly perceived to have a crucial influence on how children develop both as individuals and as members of our society. But what do we actually mean by the term 'family' and precisely how do we gauge the role that family plays in children's development? These are themes that the extracts within this chapter will help you to reflect upon. In so doing the chapter will revisit some of the themes raised in Chapter 3 when the impact of the social context on a child's development was noted. This chapter focuses on the social context that is the family and considers principally the affective impact of the family on development by looking at the theory of attachment but also alludes to some of the cognitive aspects. In much of the research and literature about family the focus is more specifically on relationships with parents and in particular the mother, but this ignores other relationships within families that are potentially important. The third extract in the chapter focuses therefore on the role of sibling relationships in development. It is also important to recognise the place of the family within a broader cultural context and this is explored in the final extract.

As a practitioner there is a strong rationale for considering the role of the family in development. Within the new Early Years Foundation Stage (DfES, 2007) 'positive relationships' are highlighted as one of the four guiding themes for practitioners and it is quite explicitly stated that: 'Children learn to be strong and independent from a base of loving and secure relationships with parents and/or a key person.'

Elaborating on this theme, the guidance for the new curriculum stresses that a:

> *Close working between early years practitioners and parents is vital for the identification of children's learning needs and to ensure a quick response to any area of particular difficulty. Parents and families are central to a child's well-being and practitioners should support this important relationship by sharing information and offering support to learning in the home.* (p.10)

Similarly, the Standards for the Early Years Professional Status (CWDC, 2007) devote four of the 39 standards to relationships with parents and carers, including Standard 29, which specifically requires practitioners to demonstrate how they:

> *Recognise and respect the influential and enduring contribution that families and parents/carers can make to children's development, well-being and learning.* (CWDC, 2007)

The ways in which parents can contribute to development is summarised by Langston, who highlights four broad areas: emotional nurture; social companionship; cognitive and language stimulation; and the care that is provided in order to promote physical and mental health and well-being (Langston, 2006, p9). As you read through the extracts covered in this chapter you may wish to ask yourself which, if any, of these areas do they focus upon and to what extent do you feel these aspects are interlinked?

Setting the scene: defining the family

Take a few moments to try to define the term 'family'. Though a superficially easy task, this can prove quite difficult, particularly if you are asked to come up with a workable definition within a group of other people. You will probably start from the model provided by your own family but often after only a few minutes' conversation with the others you will appreciate the very different forms that a family can take.

Das Gupta (1995) suggests that family structure may be grouped under one of five headings: conjugal nuclear; non-conjugal nuclear; lone parent; reconstituted (step-families); extended. You may like to follow up Das Gupta's definitions and consider how sufficient and inclusive these categories are. Try drawing up your own list of possible family types that you have come across or know to exist.

As well as acknowledging the diversity of family life it is also important to bear in mind that the family is not a static concept either for individual families or within society in general. As Draper and Duffy (2006) point out 'Families are changing, as they always have done. Parents are not an homogenous group' (p.151).

Of course it is one thing to acknowledge at a rational level that families are not homogenous or easily accommodated within a single accepted definition, but it is not always so easy to personally acknowledge the internal model of the family that you almost certainly hold. So, as you read through the rest of the chapter mentally question not only the models or definitions of the family and family relationships that the various authors appear to hold, but constantly reflect also on how your own idea of the family is contributing to your evaluation of the material presented.

Attachment theory

One of the most famous theories seeking to consider the effects of parenting on children's development is attachment theory. The theory was first elaborated by John Bowlby in the 1950s and is a theory that is principally focused on the bonds between the parents, more specifically the mother, and children that are forged during infancy and early childhood. Having explored the nature of these and of how they develop, the theory also makes claims about the likely long-term effects of the strength of these bonds on the subsequent development of the child in later life.

Attachment is seen to have a biological basis, with infants exhibiting what Bowlby calls 'proximity maintaining behaviours' (Bowlby, 1969) and he highlights the occurrence of 'separation anxiety' that can be observed in infants aged between 6 and 18 months as further evidence for the importance of attachment between infants and their special people, especially the mother.

It is a theory that has permeated quite widely into our cultural expectations of childhood and the notion of a special bond between mother and child seems to resonate with our intuitive concept of this relationship. It can therefore seem a very plausible theory. However, the theory has some potentially profound implications for individual families and society a whole. What happens if a child and his/her mother do not, for whatever reason, form a strong and lasting attachment? If the relationship between mother and child in infancy is so vital, then what does this mean for a society where increasing numbers of children are receiving childcare outside of the home in their early years? The following extract from Bowlby focuses on the specific element of his theories that crystallised these dilemmas – the theory of maternal deprivation. It is likely that you will find yourself reacting quite strongly to this extract, whether you are inclined to agree or to disagree with the propositions within it. As you read the extract try to surmount your instinctive reactions and to think about how you might offer some reasoned arguments for both standpoints.

EXTRACT ONE

Bowlby, J. (1953) Child care and the growth of love. *London: Penguin, pp11–12*

Some Causes of Mental Ill-health

What is believed to be essential for mental health is that the infant and young child should experience a warm, intimate, and continuous relationship with his mother (or permanent mother-substitute – one person who steadily 'mothers' him) in which both find satisfaction and enjoyment. It is this complex, rich, and rewarding relationship with the mother in early years, varied in countless ways by relations with the father and with the brothers and sisters, that child psychiatrists and many others now believe to underlie the development of character and of mental health.

A state of affairs in which the child does not have this relationship is termed 'maternal deprivation'. This is a general term covering a number of different situations. Thus, a child is deprived even though living at home if his mother (or permanent mother-substitute) is unable to give him the loving care small children need. Again, a child is deprived if for any reason he is removed from his mother's care. This deprivation will be relatively mild if he is then looked after by someone whom he has already learned to know and trust, but may be considerable if the foster-mother even though loving is a stranger. All these arrangements, however, give the child some satisfaction and are therefore examples of 'partial deprivation'. They stand in contrast to the almost 'complete deprivation' which is still not uncommon in institutions, residential nurseries, and hospitals, where the child often has no one person who cares for him in a personal way and with whom he may feel secure.

POINTS TO CONSIDER

- *How does this theory fit with/challenge your own experience or beliefs? Can you think of specific examples that would either support or challenge Bowlby's ideas?*

- *How might practice within an Early Years setting be designed so as to take into account the importance of a children having a relationship with 'someone whom he has already learned to know and trust'?*

- *What other potentially significant relationships does Bowlby overlook?*

- *To what extent do you think that the quality and dynamics of family relationships in early childhood impact on a child's later life?*

- *You may wish to read more of Bowlby's work in order to flesh out his theory and to follow the ways in which his theories have been refined over the past half century or so. It would also be useful to read the accounts of other researchers within this tradition, in particular the work of Mary Ainsworth (Ainsworth et al., 1978)*

Challenging Bowlby's ideas

The fact that a theory is controversial or has profound implications for important aspects of life does not of itself undermine a theory. Having said that, given the strong claims made by Bowlby's theory it is not surprising that there have been very many evaluations and critiques of his ideas. Perhaps the most famous challenge to Bowlby's ideas came from Michael Rutter. The extract from Rutter that follows has been specifically selected because it provides a good example of how theory and ideas relating to child development may be critiqued in a balanced and carefully reasoned way even when the subject matter is potentially contentious. As you read the idea make notes on not only which of Bowlby's ideas are being supported or challenged but also on the nature of the argument that Rutter is employing at each point. Is his argument based on a methodological point? Is it to do with the logical connections that are made between ideas, for example confusing a relationship between factors with the notion that one aspect thereby has a cause-and-effect relationship with another? Is it based on findings from elsewhere? Is it related to factors, or relationships between different factors, that Bowlby may have failed to consider?

EXTRACT TWO

Rutter, M. (1972) **Maternal deprivation reassessed.** *Harmondsworth: Penguin, pp19, 24–25*

Attachment

There is good evidence that most children develop strong attachments to their parents (Ainsworth 1963, 1964 Schaffer and Emerson, 1964). In his extensive review of the topic, Bowlby (1969) points to the universal occurrence of attachment behaviour in both man and subhuman primates. It may be accepted that this is a fundamental characteristic of the mother–child relationship. However, it is equally clear that there is great individual variation in the strength distribution of attachments; the main bond is not always with the mother and bonds are often multiple. Thus, Schaffer and Emerson (1964) found that the sole principal attachment was to the mother in only half of the eighteen-month-old children they studied and in nearly a third of cases the main attachment was to the father. Although there was usually one particularly strong attachment, the majority of the children showed multiple attachments of varying intensity. It may be concluded that attachment is an important, perhaps crucial, aspect of the mother–child, relationship, but equally it is a characteristic shared with other relationships.

Bowlby (1969) has argued that there is a bias for a child to attach himself especially to one figure (a characteristic he has called 'monotropy') and that this main attachment differs in kind from attachments to other subsidiary figures. However, there is a lack of supporting evidence for this claim; Schaffer (1971) has concluded that Bowlby's view is not borne out by the facts and that the breadth of attachments is largely determined by the social setting. The issue remains unsettled and requires further study.

An unbroken relationship

The main reasons for regarding continuity as an essential requisite of mothering are the well-established associations between 'broken homes' and delinquency . . ., and the short-term disturbance which often follows a young child's separation from his parents (Yarrow, 1964). Both of these findings suggest that breaks in the parent–child relationship may have adverse effects, but as breaks are frequently associated with other adverse factors it remains to be established whether it is the separation as such which is the deleterious influence (this issue is discussed further in later chapters).

That transient separations are not necessarily a bad thing is evident from the high rate of separations in normal individuals. Douglas, Ross and Simpson (1968), in a national sample of some five thousand children, showed that by four and a half years of age, a third of children had been separated from their mother for at least one week. Furthermore, they showed that there was only a weak association between brief separations and delinquency (forty-one per cent separations in delinquents as against thirty-two per cent in controls). Of course, all children must separate from their parents sometime if they are to develop independent personalities, so the question is not whether children should separate from their mothers but rather when and how separations should occur. The finding that certain sorts of happy separation may actually protect young children from the adverse effects of later stressful separation (Stacey, Dearden, Pill and Robinson, 1970) also empasizes the importance of considering the circumstances of a separation when deciding whether it is likely to be beneficial or harmful.

Perhaps an even more crucial point is the equation of 'separation' with 'discontinuity' in a relationship. In his 1951 monograph, Bowlby argued that the young pre-school child is unable to maintain a relationhip with a person in their absence and that for this reason even brief separations disrupt a relationship. Experience with normal children suggests that this is not always so, at least in favourable circumstances. Of course, young children do find it more difficult, but it seems probable that environmental conditions as well as age influence, a child's ability to maintain a bond during a person's absence. As the point is vital to the whole argument on continuity it deserves greater attention than it has received.

- *In what ways does this extract*
  - a) *Extend or develop Bowlby's ideas?*
  - b) *Challenge Bowlby's ideas?*
- *How does Rutter's contribution provide ideas that could be accommodated with EY practice?*
- *Having read the extracts from both Bowlby and Rutter, how do you now view the role of attachment in children's development?*

Notwithstanding the valid critiques of attachment theory such as that provided by Rutter, the theory has been very important and has had great influence on practice in the care and education of young children and their families. The key worker system in many Early Years settings clearly has resonance with the theory of attachment and after publication of Bowlby's original ideas many of the practices around childbirth and care of children in hospitals was restructured to reflect the importance he attributed to child–parent bonds. Before moving away from the theory of attachment it is important to acknowledge that the theory has been further developed and slightly refined over the years by Bowlby himself and by other researchers. It is equally important to note that although critiques such as that of Rutter have served to move the debate forward, the theoretical area still retains the capacity to provoke controversy. In 2006 a group of respected academics rekindled the debate yet again, as the following quote from a letter they sent to the *Daily Telegraph* demonstrates:

> *It is time for an urgent national debate on how to ensure that children receive the most appropriate care if their mothers are at work. Consistent, continuous care by a trusted figure is the key to providing a secure and nurturing environment for very young children. Research shows that its absence a can lead to behavioural difficulties in children as they grow older.* (Daily Telegraph, 21.10.06)

In this context it is clearly vital that as Early Years practitioners and students you know about the theory and are able to critique it, seeing both its strengths and limitations, and you will be able to do this with greater authenticity if you have read the original sources for yourself.

POINTS TO CONSIDER

The theory of attachment is one amongst a number of theoretical perspectives that have focused on the parental role in shaping a child's current understandings and/or their future development. Some other perspectives that you might find useful to follow up include:

- The work of Baumrind (1971), around different parental styles and children's subsequent socialisation.
- Psychoanalytical accounts of how the relationships between parents and children are instrumental in the formation of identity (Winnicott, 1971).

- From a cognitive perspective, the work of Rogoff (1990), already noted in Chapter 3 of this book, considers the notion of 'guided participation' between children and their carers.

- So-called transactional theories of development (Sameroff, 1991). In contrast to some of the ideas already encountered in this chapter, the model of parental influence is much less linear in transactional theories. Instead they acknowledge that the behaviours, attitude and temperament of the child will also have a dynamic role to play in the relationship that will in turn affect how the adult will act and this will impinge on the child's future responses. Thus the relationship is not simply a process from adult to child but a more complex and continually interactive process.

Other relationships within the family

You may well have been struck so far, and in your wider reading around the subject of early childhood, by the emphasis that seems to be placed on the mother–child relationship. Clearly the family is a much more complex web of relationships, yet you will probably find that you struggle to find significant research studies around, say, the roles of fathers, grandparents, etc. Why do you think this might be? Do you think that it reflects a cultural emphasis on the role of the mother and, if so, what is the underlying basis of that cultural emphasis? Thinking about your own practice, too, how much of your 'interaction with parents' is actually 'interactions with mothers'? Again, why do you think this might be so? Does it matter if this is the case?

Unfortunately there is still a relatively small amount of work on paternal relationships and even less in relation to the role of grandparents, though some sources for further investigation are given at the end of the chapter. Our attention will now turn to one of the family relationships that has begun to be investigated more systematically; that is, sibling relationships. One of the principal authors in this regard has been Judy Dunn. As you read the extract from Dunn you may like to reflect on your relationships with your own brothers or sisters, if you have any, or on the interactions that you have observed between brothers and sisters that you have worked with in an Early Years setting.

Dunn, J. (1984) Sisters and brothers. *London: Fontana, pp14–15*

Most children grow up with siblings – 80 per cent in the USA and Europe. The time they spend together in these early years is often far greater than the time that they spend with their mothers or their fathers. In many cultures children are brought up by their siblings: from the age of one or two they are nursed, fed, disciplined and played with by a brother or sister only three or four years older than they. It is the beginning of a relationship that lasts a lifetime – longer, indeed, than that of marriage, or of parent and child. Our first theme concerns the question of how this experience of growing up with siblings affects a child's personality, the way he or she thinks about himself, his family and friends, his intelligence, and his ways of thinking and talking.

EXTRACT THREE *continued*

On commonsense grounds it seems very likely that it may be important. Some psychologists argue, and parents would surely agree, that what children feel about, and learn from other children can dramatically influence their development. Children are particularly likely to attend to, and understand the feelings and the point of view of their friends. When children talk to, and argue with adults, they are at an obvious disadvantage: the way they see the world is different, their power and status and their understanding are limited, compared with those of adults. But between children there is greater equality. They are more likely to understand how other people who are children like themselves think or see things.

If we are to discover whether siblings do influence each other, and why it is that siblings differ so much from one another – the point that is so obvious to parents, and now is carefully documented by scientists – then we clearly have to look both at the way parents treat their different children and at the way the children relate to one another. It could well be that children themselves influence each other in ways that increase the differences between them. One child may feel hostile towards, and irritated with his sister, jealous of her relationship with their parents, infuriated by her personality and her habits. His sister in contrast may be happy and easy-going about competing for parental attention, admiring of her brother's skills, eager to please, yet rebuffed when she tries. Growing up within the same family means something very different for the two: for one child the family includes someone who arouses irritation and takes parental attention and love, for the other there is someone to admire, care about, and learn from. And of course differences in how the children behave towards one another may be closely linked to differences in how the parents treat the different children, either as a cause or as a consequence of the sibling's behaviour.

If siblings do influence one another directly, it may not be that the influence is always to increase the differences between them. Siblings may admire, imitate and identify with one another, uniting in the face of problems and difficulties, emulating the qualities they like about each other. The point is that if we are to understand how patterns of personality develop, we must not ignore the possible influence of the children with whom individuals grow up and with whom they spend their early years – their sisters and brothers.

POINTS TO CONSIDER

- *Can you relate specific examples from you own experiences and/or practice to the themes that Dunn raises?*

- *What are the implications of these ideas for you as a practitioner in Early Years? How do you build on the strengths of the sibling relationship yet militate against some of the less positive effects?*

- *This extract from Dunn focuses on the more affective influences that siblings may have one on another's development. Elsewhere in the same book, which you would find an interesting read, Dunn emphasises how children's cognitive and social understanding may be enhanced by the sibling relationship. Can you think of some ways in which this might be so and/or give some examples from your own experience?*

> ### POINTS TO CONSIDER
>
> - Another strand of Dunn's work around siblings has been to consider the effects of birth order within a family and to consider the implications for older siblings when a new baby arrives in the family. Again think about your own experiences. What do you think these effects might be? You could follow up these ideas by reading other examples of Judy Dunn's work that are suggested at the end of the chapter.
>
> - Reflect on the links between the cognitive support that brothers and sisters may provide for one another and the social aspects of learning that have been covered elsewhere in this book (Chapter 3).
>
> - You may wish to consider the similarities and differences between sibling relationships and other peer relationships including friendships. Howe (1996) offers a particularly useful synopsis of some of the developmental advantages of early friendships. These include evidence of more complex play between friends, which facilitates the development of a representative rather than literal way of thinking about their world.

Considering the family relationships together

One of the main points that Dunn has demonstrated through her work on the nature of the sibling relationship is the way in which the relationships between siblings is itself mediated by the quality and pattern of the other relationships within the family.

This may seem self-evident but it can be all too easy to become so focused on a particular relationship, whether that of mother–child or sibling–sibling, and so forget that these do not exist in a social vacuum but form part of a more complex and shifting web of relationships. Think about your own family and the ways in which on different days and at different times in your life the relationships with different family members may change. Did you become closer to your mother when you had children? As a child did you find that you could row with your brother or sister one moment only to ally yourself with them later on the day against your parents? There are many possible examples: at both major and minor life points relationships are fluid rather than static and driven by a range of contextual factors.

Systems Theory

One way of attempting to conceptualise this interconnectedness and multiplicity of influences is systems theory. According to Schaffer (2004, pp. 88–9) this is based on the following set of principles:

- Wholeness, whereby a system is an organised whole that is greater then the sum of its parts.
- Integrity of systems, whereby the system as a whole is composed of subsystems that are related to one another.
- Circularity of influence, whereby all of the components within the system are interdependent; a change in one has implications for the others.

- Stability and change, whereby systems can be affected by outside influences, and change in one component means change in all of the others and in the relationships between them.

On the face of it this can seem a rather mechanistic model, but try to find some real-life family examples to fit each of the different aspects and you will find it comes to life. You might incidentally find it a useful framework for analysing other complex relationships, e.g. the organisation and working of an Early Years setting.

The family in context

If it is problematic to focus simplistically on particular relationships within a family without some concept of the wider family whole, might it not also be problematic to focus on the family as if it is somehow divorced from the outside world? Indeed in the description of systems theory it was suggested that the family might well be impacted by events and contexts beyond itself. You can no doubt think of any number of particular events or occurrences that could serve to alter the dynamics and relationships between family members. What may be less easy to do is to consider how a family and its individual members may be affected by the outside world on an ongoing and possibly unremarked basis.

In the extract that follows Bronfenbrenner describes a view of society in which individuals and their development are seen as 'nested' in a series of broader structures. This includes the home, or family, but also factors that one might think of as far beyond the home such as government policy. As you read the extract think about the many ways in which a child within a family may be affected by a broader range of phenomena and societal structures and relationships.

EXTRACT FOUR

Bronfenbrenner, U. (1979) **The ecology of human development. Experiments by nature and design.** *Cambridge, MA: Harvard University Press, pp3–4*

I offer a new theoretical perspective for research in human development. The perspective is new in its conception of the developing person, of the environment, and especially of the evolving interaction between the two. Thus development is defined in this work as a lasting change in the way in which a person perceives and deals with his environment. For this reason, it is necessary at the outset to give an indication of the somewhat unorthodox concept of the environment presented in this volume. Rather than begin with a formal exposition, I shall first introduce this concept by some concrete examples.

The ecological environment is conceived as a set of nested structures, each inside the next, like a set of Russian dolls. At the innermost level is the immediate setting containing the developing person. This can be the home, the classroom, or as often happens for research purposes – the laboratory or the testing room. So far we appear to be on familiar ground (although there is more to see than has thus far

EXTRACT FOUR continued

met the investigator's eye). The next step, however, already leads us off the beaten track for it requires looking beyond single settings to the relations between them. I shall argue that such interconnections can be as decisive for development as events taking place within a given setting. A child's ability to learn to read in the primary grades may depend no less on how he is taught than on the existence and nature of ties between the school and the home.

The third level of the ecological environment takes us yet farther afield and evokes a hypothesis that the person's development is profoundly affected by events occurring in settings in which the person is not even present. I shall examine data suggesting that among the most powerful influences affecting the development of young children in modern industrialized societies are the conditions of parental employment.

Finally, there is a striking phenomenon pertaining to settings at all three levels of the ecological environment outlined above: within any culture or subculture, settings of a given kind – such as homes, streets, or offices – tend to be very much alike, whereas between cultures they are distinctly different. It is as if within each society or subculture there existed a blueprint for the organization of every type of setting. Furthermore, the blueprint can be changed, with the result that the structure of the settings in a society can become markedly altered and produce corresponding changes in behavior and development. For example, research results suggest that a change in maternity ward practices affecting the relation between mother and new-born can produce effects still detectable five years later. In another case, a severe economic crisis occurring in a society is seen to have positive or negative impact on the subsequent development of children throughout the life span, depending on the age of the child at the time that the family suffered financial duress.

POINTS TO CONSIDER

- *List as many as possible factors outside of the family that could have a developmental influence on the family and the individuals within it.*

- *Bronfenbrenner suggests that the time or era into which one is born may also have an influence on the family and individual development. Thinking back over the last 100 years, think of ways in which the notions of what it is to be a child and of the family may have changed.*

- *If cultural context is an important element in determining the expectations of the family and of the child, what are the implications for you as a practitioner?*

Cross-cultural patterns in relation to families and development

Rogoff (2003) takes this idea of a cultural dimension to family and development further and contends that we can only understand the development of individuals 'in the light of the cultural practices and circumstances of their experiences' (pp.3–4). In a fascinating book, listed at the end of this chapter, she explores some of the ways this is manifested in different cultural and family practices around the world. She rightly acknowledges that it would be erroneous to assume that everyone or every family within a certain cultural milieu will act in a uniform way, but she highlights the ways in which interactions within families may be very different according to dominant cultural traditions. Some societies, for example, may encourage children to be part of the ongoing adult life of the community whereas other societies may see childhood as a state that is and should be more separate from adulthood. The types of expectations and rules for social interaction may also vary – is it considered appropriate, for example, for a child to question something an adult had told them? You may like to think of some other examples where cultural expectations and norms may be very different.

In a similar, if less global, vein the work of Brooker (2002) highlights how family expectations of schooling and education may be very different based on differing cultural expectations. Focusing on the experiences of children and their families from different cultural backgrounds as they transfer to school, Brooker shows how settings may have dominant expectations, or practices, that do not necessarily accord with the expectations of families. One example is the arguably dominant discourse amongst Early Years practitioners of the importance of play for learning in the Early Years and yet for some families the expectation may be that school is supposed to be about 'work'. If not addressed by practitioners then the dissonance between family and school expectations may result in difficulties for the child's experiences of school. Brooker explicitly draws on the work of Bourdieu around 'cultural capital', which suggests that children from middle-class families may be advantaged when it comes to formal schooling since the cultural environment of the home is more similar to that of the school than that of children from working-class families.

C H A P T E R   S U M M A R Y

The extracts within this chapter have ranged from a close scrutiny of the role of the mother–child bond to the broad sweep of Bronfenbrenner's work, in which the family and the individuals within it are set firmly within a broader social and cultural context. Along the way you have considered how 'family' can be defined and looked in detail at the highly influential theory of attachment. The critique of this theory offered by Rutter will have alerted you to the ways in which important theories can be evaluated and where necessary challenged.

You have been encouraged to reflect on the extent to which it is appropriate to focus on particular relationships within the family and/or the more complex interplay between different individuals within a family, or indeed between the family and the wider socio-cultural context. Your day-to-day experience may seem rather more real than some of the 'high theory' but precisely because family is something we all have direct experience of and opinions about, it is important to be aware of the different theoretical ideas about family. In so doing we may be able to think more objectively about the potentially varied experiences of the families with whom we work, and to further appreciate how significant those family experiences may be for the children in our care.

REFERENCES

Bowlby, J. (1953) *Child care and the growth of love*. London: Penguin.

Bowlby, J. (1969) *Attachment and loss. Vol. 1 Attachment*. London: Hogarth Press.

Bronfenbrenner, U. (1979) *The ecology of human development. Experiments by nature and design*. Cambridge, MA. Harvard University Press.

Brooker, L. (2002) *Starting school – Young children learning cultures*. Buckingham: Open University Press.

CWDC (2007) *Guidance to the standards for the award of Early Years Professional Status*. Leeds: CWDC.

Das Gupta, P. (1995) Growing up in families, in P. Barnes *Personal, social and emotional development of children*. Oxford: Blackwell/Open University.

DfES (2007) Early Years Foundation Stage, www.standards.dfes.gov.uk/eyfs/site/index.htm Accessed 27.03.07.

Draper, L. and Duffy, B. (2006) Working with parents, in G. Pugh and B. Duffy *Contemporary issues in the early years* (4th edn). London: Sage.

Dunn, J. (1984) *Sisters and brothers*. London: Fontana.

Langston, A. (2006) Why parents matter, in L. Abbott and A. Langston *Parents matter. Supporting the Birth to Three Matters Framework*. Maidenhead: McGraw-Hill Education.

Rogoff, B. (1990) *Apprenticeship in thinking*. Oxford: Oxford University Press .

Rogoff, B. (2003) *The cultural nature of human development*. Oxford: Oxford University Press.

Rutter, M. (1972) *Maternal deprivation reassessed*. London: Penguin.

Schaffer, H.R. (2004) *Child psychology*. Oxford: Blackwell Publishing.

FURTHER READING

Ainsworth, M., Blehar, M.C., Waters, E. and Wall, S. (1978) *Patterns of attachment: a psychological study of the strange situation*. Hillsdale, NJ: Lawrence Ehrlbaum.

Baumrind, D. (1971) Current patterns of parental authority, *Developmental Psychology Monographs* 1, 1–103.

Dunn, J. and Kendrick, C. (1982) *Siblings: Love, envy and understanding.* London: Grant McIntyre.

Howe, C. (1996) The earliest friendships, in Bukowski, W.M., Newcomb, A.F. and Hartup, W.W. *The company they keep. Friendship in childhood and adolescence*. Cambridge: Cambridge University Press.

Sameroff, A.J. (1991) The social context of development, in M. Woodhead, R. Carr and P. Light (eds) *Becoming a person*. Abingdon: Routledge.

Winnicott, D.W. (1971) *Playing and reality*. London: Pelican Books.

Chapter 6
Listening to children in the Early Years

Rachel Friedman

OBJECTIVES

By the end of this chapter you should have:
- further considered why listening to the voice of children is more than just hearing and recording children;
- critically evaluated what role is given to children's voice in settings you have visited or in your work setting;
- analysed how your own voice informs the meaning you make of the voice of children.

Professional Standards for EYPS: S15, S18, S26, S27, S28

As you work through this chapter you might find it useful to keep a journal of conversations among children and between children and adults. Furthermore it will be useful to think about the following questions:

1. What was the prevailing attitude towards children when you were growing up? Can you remember an experience as a child when your views were either ignored or listened to?

2. Consider what you know about the United Nations Convention on the Rights of the Child (UNCRC). What impact has the UNCRC had in your life?

Introduction

No doubt by now you have had numerous opportunities to go out into the field with the purpose of observing young children doing what most young children do best – interacting with others and with their environment. You have probably spent hours watching, taking notes and documenting conversations between children and between children and adults. You will have amassed in your observation journal entries that demonstrate children being kind to each other, children hurting others, children working out conflict either alone or with an adult's help and prompting. You might have worked in an environment where children or adults have assembled a list of class rules. You will have hopefully observed or worked in a setting where children have had an active role in influencing the curriculum or a portion thereof. All of these are examples of practical ways in which the voices of young children are heard.

What do we do with the seemingly extraneous children's voices that we hear, those that are not part of our focused plans? How do we use them? Are they private or are they meant to be shared between adults? And if we record them, to whom do they belong; what are the ethical issues involved in using these voices? What weight do we give children's voices in our setting? in our curriculum? How do these voices differ from other kinds of voices – the ones that children intentionally choose to share? The voices that have another message in them?

In this chapter issues around children's voices will be explored. We will start the discussion by looking at the rules that govern our behaviours and guide us in our work with young children. The United Nation's Convention on the Rights of the Child (UN, 1989) is the document that was developed to ensure that the rights of a vulnerable layer of the population are protected. The UNCRC applies to children all over the globe. We will then take a look at the local guidance that is used by those engaged in working with young children and their families. Currently the two guiding documents are *Birth to Three Matters* (2005) and *Curriculum Guidance for the Foundation Stage* (2000), which has now been superseded by the new *Early Years Foundation Stage*, published in March 2007. Understanding the guidance, whether local or international, will help you understand the material that follows.

In the following section we will explore the work of people who are engaged in working with young children and their families. The authors chosen are active in supporting the 'voices' of young children. There are distinct differences in the manner in which these authors work. They work in different countries, they work with different age ranges within early childhood, and they focus on different aspects of the experience of being a young child. What links the authors is that all of the experiences are based around Early Years settings and give voice to the young child and their experiences and understanding of the world.

The Mosaic approach to listening to young children (Clark and Moss, 2001) comes from the practice of working with the youngest children who are being cared for outside of their homes. As the name suggests, the Mosaic approach views 'listening' as a multi-method and 'voice' as not limited to the sounds that are emitted from the throat. The next work explored is that of Vivian Paley, a USA early childhood educator. She has authored numerous books narrating the experiences of young children in their settings. In Paley's books children's voices are heard through work that engages children in dictating and staging short stories. The work of Angela Anning and Kathy Ring (2004) is drawn upon to describe attempts to give a voice to children through their drawings. This body of work also focuses on the relationships between home and school. Through the literature of Elfer *et al.* (2003) we will explore the consideration for the voice of the child through the key-person approach in the nursery. The final exploration of children and voice will bring us to the work of Van Ausdale and Feagin (2001). These two authors explored children's understanding of race and racism through listening to the conversations of children in pre-school.

Setting the stage: What listening to young children means to me ...

When working on issues that may challenge previous understanding, knowledge and experience it is often suggested that there is a need to first explore one's own beliefs (Jacobson, 2003). Listening to children, not just for hearing what children are saying, but rather listening so that the meanings of their messages can resonate in their environment, seems like it might provide a challenge to the way we might think about the role of children in the Early Years or in the Early Years setting.

> **SCENARIO**
>
> *The practitioners in the Blue Room meet each week to plan their weekly lessons for their 4- and 5-year olds. At the end of each meeting the team produces a detailed daily plan outlining each activity in all of the areas of learning. Each Monday morning a new programme starts. One Tuesday morning in October Sam arrives and announces that his new sister arrived that morning. The Blue Room practitioners, knowing that Sam's mother was not pregnant, briefly acknowledge Sam's news and continue with their scheduled programme. Sam continues to share his 'news' with all of the children and parents that will listen to him. At circle time he dominates the conversation, finally announcing that he would get the pictures from his jacket pocket. Sam produces the pictures of himself sitting under a banner reading 'welcome home Mum and Baby Sis' in which he is wearing the same clothes that he is wearing to school. The Blue Room practitioners are surprised.*

Why do you think the practitioners behaved in the manner described above? Could you imagine that you might act towards Sam as did the practitioners in the scenario? How might you have responded to Sam had you been a practitioner in the Blue Room? Was Sam's message heard by the practitioners in the setting? Listening to children is not a passive activity; it is not simply hearing their words. What should have happened in the Blue Room that morning?

UNCRC

A common starting place for discussing the voice of the young child is Articles 12 and 13 of the United Nations Convention on the Rights of the Child (UNCRC) (UNHRC, 1989). The United Kingdom ratified the UNCRC in 1991. By ratifying the convention, citizens of the United Kingdom are obligated to work according to the articles of the convention. Furthermore, governments have an obligation to make the convention known to both adults and children (UNCRC, Article 42).

Look at the website **www.unicef.org.uk/youthvoice/rights.asp**; this website is UNICEF's website for children and young people. On this site you will find a summary of the UNCRC written in child-friendly language. Compare how Articles 12 and 13 appear in their abbreviated formats and their full-length formats. How might you talk with practitioners and other adults about listening to children? How might you talk with young children about the power of their voices?

> ## *Article 12*
>
> 1. *You have the right to say what you think should happen when adults are making decisions that affect you, and to have your opinions taken into account.*
>   **www.unicef.org.uk/youthvoice/pdfs/uncrc.pdf**

Guidance

Birth to Three Matters (Sure Start, 2002) was until March 2007 the framework available for those working with the youngest children, and has informed the more recently published *Early Years Foundation Stage* (2007). When considering the voice of the child for this age group we must not limit our understanding of this concept to just 'voice'; rather we must pay attention to the whole child. Although the guidance attempts to mimic a curriculum by having 'aspects' and 'components', the guidance also recognises its own limitations: 'The Framework ... informs and develops practice whilst acknowledging that working with babies and children is a complex, challenging and demanding task and that often there are no easy answers' (Sure Start, 2002, p.4). By adopting a holistic approach to working with babies and toddlers, practitioners rely on their relationship with families, carers and their own interactions in order to ensure that the voices of the youngest children are heard.

Mosaic approach

The Mosaic approach was developed as a result of a 'search ... for a way to listen to young children [talk] about their own lives' (Clark and Moss, 2001, p.11). This approach aims to find ways in which children's voices are not only heard but also empowered. The Mosaic approach was developed from work with three- and four-year old children; however, it has been adapted for work with a range of children and adults.

In order for children's voices to be heard, guidelines must be in place. The components of the guidelines are 'multi-method, participatory, reflexive, adaptable, focused on children's lived experiences, and embedded into practice' (ibid., p.5). Use of the term 'multi-method' takes into account that the voice of the child need not be an oral voice; rather it might be visual, kinaesthetic or experiential. All of these expressions of the child should be taken into account. 'Participatory' refers to the child being central to the experience. 'Reflexivity', unlike when the doctor checks our reflexes, demands a more active role; we hear, see, experience, and then we reflect. Again there is confusion about reflexivity in practice; being reflexive is being active although the activity may be difficult for those outside of the experience to see. Reflexivity involves an engagement with an idea, a concept, conversation, and then time is needed to consider deeply the meaning, the impact, and then there is a response or a dialogue. Reflexivity allows time to make meaning out of an action. The Mosaic approach has been created with intentional adaptability; the programme could be used by other practitioners in other settings. The experiences of the child are central because it is through these experiences that children make sense of their worlds. Children make sense of a wide range of experiences, not just those that have been intentionally designated as for children. In recognising the breadth of the experiences of the child the Mosaic approach allows for opportunities to explore the depth of these experiences. The designers of the Mosaic approach argue for the embedding of the approach in the curriculum: listening to children should not happen just between 2 and 3 in the afternoon, but rather be an integral part of the Early Years experience.

In the final chapter of the book *Listening to young children: The Mosaic approach* (Clark and Moss, 2001), the authors discuss some of the challenges of this approach. Read through the section and consider the following questions:

1. What are your beliefs about children's voice in the Early Years setting?

2. How might you introduce this approach to other members of staff?

3. Is the Mosaic approach aligned to the philosophy of early childhood settings that you have worked in or visited?

4. What other issues has the reading raised for you? How will you take the ideas presented here further?

EXTRACT ONE

Clark, A. and Moss, P. (2001) Listening to young children: The Mosaic approach. *London: National Children's Bureau, pp63–67*

Conditions of listening

What needs to be in place in order to take advantage of the Mosaic approach? Many of the factors discussed below will already be central to Early Years practice.

Climate of listening

This fundamental desire to listen to and involve children is a necessary prerequisite if children's views and experiences are going to influence the everyday relationships between adults and children in early childhood institutions.

The use of the Mosaic approach may be one way in which to help adults and young children to reflect together on this process of 'living, learning, loving and being'.

This climate of listening does not exist in a vacuum. How children are viewed at home is of course pertinent to a debate about listening to young children. Staff used group dicussions with parents to explore differences between rules, boundaries and level of choice offered to children at home and in the nursery.

Such discussions would be a useful starting point for introducing the Mosaic approach, which in turn could foster this climate of listening, in which parents', staff and young children's views are respected and differences can be debated.

Taking time to listen

Listening to young children cannot be a rushed activity. The younger the child the less able and desirable it is to rely on direct questions. The Mosaic approach involves a time commitment for Early Years staff in several ways:

- *Gathering the material will take longer because we are not relying on a single method of communication.*

- *Interpreting the material gathered is time-consuming.*

Training

Listening to young children's perspectives is a skilful task which requires awareness raising and training.

Training in child development is obviously an important prerequisite of understanding how young children communicate.

The use of the Mosaic approach also raises questions about in-service training. Staff need to feel confident in offering a range of different 'languages' for children to choose to express themselves. Specific workshops may be needed to expand the range of tools on offer in a setting.

Access by children

What conditions are needed for young children to be involved in the Mosaic approach? This study suggests that there is potential for children of different ages and abilities to participate in this way. There are possibilities of developing this framework with parents, keyworkers and older siblings of children under one year.

The flexibility of the approach also allows methods to be adapted by staff to suit the needs and interests of the yound children in care. The tools described in this report involve at least four of the areas of learning: personal, social and emotional development; communication, language and literacy; knowledge and understanding of the world, and creative development. In asking children to explore what is important to them about a setting there is the opportunity to develop new skills and thinking, which in turn enables children to achieve their Early Learning Goals.

Storytelling

Vivian Gussin Paley was an early childhood teacher for many years. Although now retired from teaching she has continued to engage with young children through her work with teachers and writing books. She is the author of numerous books that address a wide range of topics about Early Years education.

Paley is best known for her use of story in her work with young children. In her classes the children had opportunities to dictate their own stories and then to act them out with their classmates. After attending an evening presentation that she gave to the practitioners in my town, I too adopted this practice in my class for 4- and 5-year olds. During the evening session Paley modelled a manner in which she might take dictation from a young child. The opportunity for a practitioner to choose to make the time to put all other activities aside and to listen to a child, in the course of a typical early childhood session, is a rather empowering action.

In the extract below Paley tells the reader that as a novice teacher she had a view very different from the one that she eventually came to adopt.

Paley, V.G. (2004) A child's work: The importance of fantasy play. Chicago, IL: University of Chicago, pp16–19

Nearly everything in my training as a teacher led me to believe that the questions were supposed to come from me. Preoccupied by my own questions. I did not perceive that the books I so eagerly read to the children were not the only or even the primary source of stories in the classroom. The children were, in fact, natural-born storytellers who created literature as easily as I turned the pages of a book.

It was not that I doubted the children's seriousness, but I did not follow their words as I would those of a novelist or a playwright. The Brontës must have rehearsed similar themes as they played on the moors of west Yorkshire, yet I gave no thought to such possibilities. I could see that the children's play promoted a long list of social, emotional, verbal, and physical skills that could be reported in a fairly straightforward manner. However, I skipped over the end result, a phenomenon not as easy to capture on a checklist. The children were inventing stories that sounded as if they came from an earlier place in the common narrative, from the first rungs on the ladder of storytelling.

'Pretend I'm your baby dinosaur and I'm lost,' a child might say, 'and then you call me but I don't come because I have a different name now and then you hear a noise and you think it's a wolf but you can't call me because you don't know my name now.'

This child knows how to play, I would note. She is able to include other children and thus be a friend. But I would pass over the story the child had imagined and the questions of identity being posed. Furthermore, the previous day it may have been the mother dinosaur who was lost and the baby who searched. Roles were constantly being switched and stories unraveled and reissued in different forms, but I confused the extraordinary with the mundane.

Even when I overheard conversations that were startling and profound I seldom recognized the uniqueness of this activity that so preoccupied the children. 'Pretend I'm a big sister just like you,' said a little girl, climbing out of a doll-corner crib. 'I'm not a baby anymore. I'm you!'

'No! don't pretend that!' cautioned her playmate, suddenly remorseful, stepping out of her role. 'Don't be like me! Because I'm really bad!'

'Like the wolf?'

'Oh, wait, now it's okay. I'm a good sister now.'

Had I not heard these lines before? Isn't this what the older brother warns the younger brother in Long Day's Journey Into Night? *Watch out for me, Eugene O'Neill has Jamie tell Edmond, I'm no good and I'll try to bring you down to where I am. But I'm being a good brother now to tell you this.*

- *In an early childhood setting, whose questions guide the curriculum?*
- *Can you align the model of practice that Paley is advocating with the early childhood frameworks of practice that guide your practice?*

Drawing

Like Vivian Gussin Paley, Angela Anning and Kathy Ring (2004) believe that it is important to listen to children; however, the medium through which they listen to children is through drawing: 'we believe that drawing offers a powerful vehicle for hearing what young children are telling us' (ibid., p.xi). *Making sense of children's drawing* (Anning and Ring, 2004) is the story of seven children and the connections that are made between home and school, as the children learn to draw.

This longitudinal study took place over a few years. The children's stories are presented as individual case studies grounded within theory about meaning-making and the stages of learning to draw. Each child is presented within the context of their home and school setting. Read the section 'Implications for educational contexts'.

EXTRACT THREE

Anning, A. and Ring, K. (2004) Making sense of children's drawing. Maidenhead: Open University Press, pp122–124

Many practitioners remain fixed in the mindset of developmental stage theory approaches to drawing or, in the expectation that drawing must lead directly into early writing. There are few experienced trainers in the field of art education able to help practioners understand the pedagogy of drawing in supporting generalist approaches to training early years practitioners. Art specialists have been culled as the teacher and nursery officer training curriculum requirements for preparation to teach foundations subjects of the National Curriculum narrowed. Art advisers within Local Authorities have been re-deployed as inspectors of general standards. There are some good quality resources promoted by the Campaign for Drawing (www.drawingpower.org.uk), but their excellent website reaches a small proportion of practitioners. So a campaign to empower practitioners with an understanding of how drawing can support and extend young children's learning in pre-school settings is going to be challenging.

Our young children deserve better than this. We need to re-affirm the centrality of creativity in their thinking and learning. We need to recognize that multi-modality is core to their preferred ways of representing and communicating their growing understanding of the world and their roles as active members of communities. We need parents to gain confidence In their own intuitive and learned skills in becoming their children's first and most important teachers – including their capabilities in drawing. We need pratitioners who have the courage to press for a radical revision of the curriculum for young children and argue for the importance of drawing within that curriculum. We need politicians and policy makers who have the strength and humility to admit where they got some things wrong in early childhood education. We need researchers who can explore and explain the pedagogy of play and creativity and the role of drawing within playful, creative and learning behaviours. We need a society that can listen to children and recognize that perhaps their drawings may tell us much more about childhood than we ever imagined.

- *This text, like the previous one, might be seen as a challenge to some practitioners; what is your position on Anning and Rings' implications?*

- *How does this reading relate to the Paley selection? What position would you take?*

Key person approach

It is important to remember that the frameworks that guide the work of practitioners refer also to the youngest children in care outside of their family homes. Most of the authors referred to in this chapter focus their work, at least initially, on children between 3 and 5 years of age. In this section we will consider a practice that has impact for the voices of the youngest children and their families.

Our understanding of attachment comes from the work of Ainsworth and Bowlby, and is supported by more contemporary practitioners such as Stern, Leach, and Gerhardt. Bowlby (1979) is known for his work on attachment theory and Ainsworth for her 'strange situation' test (1978). Both Stern and Leach aim to write from a child-centred perspective. Stern (1990) has written extensively on the early relationship between mother and infant and Leach (1994) has written on parents, pregnancy, and childhood. Gerhardt (2004) makes the link between current understanding of brain development and the emotional development of babies. It is the work of these practitioners and others that have contributed to the 'key person' approach.

> The key person approach is a way of working in nurseries in which the whole focus and organisation is aimed at enabling and supporting close attachments between individual children and individual nursery staff. The key person approach is an involvement, an individual and reciprocal commitment between a member of staff and a family. It is an approach that has clear benefits for all involved.

(Elfer *et al.*, 2003, p18)

Elfer *et al.* do focus on the importance of the use of the terminology 'key persons' vs. 'key worker'. Perhaps we could approach this notion of the name of the role more broadly; it is the role of the key person that is important to us in our consideration of the voice of the child and not the name of the role. What are the names given to those people who are key persons in settings that you have visited? Can you describe their role?

Read the extracts below that are taken from the remainder of Chapter 2 of Elfer *et al.*, 'What is the key person approach?'

Elfer, P. et al., (2003) **Key persons in the nursery.** *London: David Fulton, pp18–21*

What is the key person approach?

The benefits of a key person approach

For babies and young children: *The key person(s) makes sure that, within the day-to-day demands of a nursery each child feels special and individual, cherished and thought about by someone in particular while they are away from home. It is as though the child were 'camped out in the key person's mind' or that there is an elastic thread of attachment that allows for being apart as well as for being together. The child in the nursery will experience a close relationship that is affectionate and reliable.*

For parents, particularly mothers: *The key person(s) approach ensures that parents have the opportunity to build a personal relationship with 'someone' rather than 'all of them' working in the nursery. The benefits are likely to be peace of mind and the possibility of building a partnership with professional staff who may share with them the pleasures and stresses of child-rearing. It gives parents the chance to liaise with someone else who is fully committed and familiar with their baby or child.*

For the key person: *The key person approach is intense, hard work and a big commitment. This relationship makes very real physical, intellectual and personal demands upon the key person and these need to be understood, the benefits of being and becoming a key person is the sense that you really matter to a child and to their family. You are likely to have a powerful impact on the child's well-being, their mental health and their chances to think and learn. These powers and responsibilities will engender feelings of pleasure and pain, the joy and relief of partings and reunions, and the satisfaction and anxiety of being a key person in a child's formative early years care and education.*

For the nursery: *The key person approach leads to better-satisfied and engaged staff, improved care and learning for the children, and a parent clientele who are likely to develop a more trusting confidence in the competencies, qualities and devotion of professional staff. There are indications that this approach reduces staff sickness and absence, and develops involvement and positive attitudes to professional development within staff teams.*

Why 'key person' and not 'key worker'

The terms 'key worker' and 'key person' are often used interchangeably in nurseries as well as in other areas of social care, for example in hospitals or in work with people with mental or physical disabilities. We would like to draw a clear distinction between the two terms. A 'key worker' is often used to describe a role in which the focus is on liaison or coordinating between different professionals or disciplines, making sure that services work in a coordinated way. It is quite different from the 'key person' role defined above. The term 'key worker' is also used to describe how staff work strategically in nurseries to enhance smooth organisation and record-keeping. This is only one part of being a key person, which is an emotional relationship as well as an organisational strategy.

EXTRACT FOUR *continued*

The key person approach for babies and young children

The first few years, and especially the first 12 months, are a very sensitive, special, exciting, anxious, often overwhelming time for a young child. If nurseries work well, they may be able to provide a deeply satisfying and enriching experience for the youngster. This is not replacing *but* supplementing *the loving care and learning time children need at home.*

As babies move towards crawling, toddling and more confident walking, they are also able to seek out the adults they need. The availability of one main adult whom they can count on is very important to them.

POINTS TO CONSIDER

- *Can you identify elements of this approach that appear to 'give voice' to children?*

- *In considering the 'key person approach'; how would you identify this kind of care? Is it child-centred? family-centred? caregiver-centred?*

- *Consider the range of approaches to care for young children that you have read about or observed; which of these models place the voice of the youngest child in the centre? Is that the appropriate place of the youngest child, when his/her voice is one that is perhaps considered not clearly heard?*

Young children and race

The first R: How children learn race and racism (Van Ausdale and Feagin, 2001) details Debi Van Ausdale's yearly venture into a pre-school setting in which she listened to conversations that were taking place between children. The book 'examine[s] when, where, and how children make use of racial and ethnic understandings and distinctions in their everyday lives' (p41).

Van Ausdale and Feagin devote an entire chapter to 'how adults view children' (pp155–174). In this chapter they present a variety of scenarios that depict 'adultcentric conviction'. There are three selections taken from this chapter. Read the section of the chapter presented below to understand how the term 'adultcentric' is explained.

When you have finished reading consider the question that follows.

EXTRACT FIVE

Van Ausdale, D. and Feagin, J.R. (2001) **How children learn race and racism,** *Lanham, MD: Rowman & Littlefield, pp159–160*

In this next account, we see a small part of one child's effort to explain her racial-ethnic background in the face of constant and predicatable adult disbelief.

A volunteer, new to the center and trying to get to know the children, approaches Corinne with a smile on her face. 'Hi!' the young woman says brightly. 'My name is Cheryl.' 'I'm Corinne,' the child replies, looking up from her play 'Want to play with me?' Corinne asks, pleased that an adult is taking an interest in her. 'Sure' replies Cheryl 'What are you doing?' 'I'm doing chemisty,' Corinnne replies 'You can watch. Cheryl smiles and settles down next to Corinne 'Where are you from?' Cheryl asks Corinne. 'Africa,' Corinne responds, glancing warily at the woman, and asks in return, 'Where are you from?' The woman responds, 'Oh, I'm from here – here in this state, that is.' Cheryl seems to regard Corinne with some amusement. 'Africa, huh. That's really interesting.' Corinne eyes her, waiting. Her experience is that most grown-ups do not believe her when she tells them where she is from, but this particular adult just lets the information go and asks, 'What kind of chemistry are you doing? Tell me about it.'

'Boy, is that little girl confused,' the volunteer offers, beginning to talk as Debi approaches the table. 'She just told me she's from Africa.' Debi smiles and begins to verify Corinne's assertion, but the young woman does not allow her to speak and continues, 'Isn't that cute? They get so mixed up. It's amazing how they twist things around, you know, mix up what they hear at home. She probably heard that she's African American.' By now Vicky has joined the group, and she interjects, 'Oh, no, Corinne's really from Africa.' Vicky names the country and adds, 'She speaks two languages too.' The volunteer, looking sheepish, replies. 'Oh, that's just so cute!' She gets up and heads for the tire swing, where she begins pushing the children.

The volunteer's assumptions about Corinne's identity illustrate how adults anticipate the extent of children's knowledge. They interpret what children do according to what the adults expect children to be able to do at particular ages and stages.

When children's behavior does not match adults' expectations, the adults adjust their evaluations to suit their preconceptions.

In their perspective, Corinne suffers from childish confusion, and this confusion must arise from some other adult's misguided attempts to teach her about her heritage. Incongruity is thus satisfactorily explained in the adults' minds. Interestingly, in this particular incident the misconception is cleared up.

However, for the most part adults are never challenged in such evaluations of children. Adultcentrism prevails.

Corinne was routinely disbelieved and corrected by newcomers who were not aware of her heritage. Teachers usually explained to newcomers that Corinne knew what she was talking about, but we never observed any of them apologize to the little girl

---

EXTRACT FIVE *continued*

or attempt to engage her in conversation about her origins. In this regard, it is significant that Corinne was the only child at the center who we observed being routinely dismissed and challenged when she discussed her origins with other people. Several other children enrolled at the school were also from foreign countries but we never witnessed an adult challenging their knowledge of national origin. Apparently, adults had no difficulty in accepting that one child is from Europe and another is from China. Adults routinely expressed interest upon learning that a young child was from another country, asking them about their families and experiences, except when that child was Corinne. Corinne's accurate and detailed stories of Africa were dismissed as confusion or fantasy. Corinne was an adept storyteller, and her stories were confirmed by her parents. Indeed, they reported that she had a sharp memory of details that even her mother and father did not recall until she reminded them. Apparently, there was an interesting interaction going on for this particular child. Her dark skin and facility with words prompted adults to dismiss her stories with much more ease.

POINTS TO CONSIDER

- *Have you ever found yourself explaining a child's behaviour using terms like 'precocious' and 'confused'?*

Read through the second extract and consider the following questions:

- What is happening to this young child as the adult attempts to make sense of the child's words and sentiments?

- Reflect back on your own history; can you recall a time when something similar happened to you? How did you respond?

C H A P T E R   S U M M A R Y

The aims of this chapter were to enable you to consider what listening to children means in a broad context; to enable you to reflect on practices that you have observed or participated in; and to spark you into thinking about your attitudes and actions reflects on the way the voice of the child is heard. Through the use of a broad range of literature the reader has been exposed to various contexts for understanding the voice of the child, its potential and the related laws governing practice.

REFERENCES

Anning, A. and Ring, K. (2004) *Making sense of children's drawing*. Maidenhead: McGraw-Hill Education.

Clark, A. and Moss, P. (2001) *Listening to young children: The Mosaic approach*. London: National Children's Bureau.

Elfer, P., Goldschmied, E. and Selleck, D. (2003) *Key persons in the nursery: Building relationships for quality provision*. London: David Fulton.

Paley, V.G. (2004) *A child's work: The importance of fantasy play*. Chicago, IL: University of Chicago.

Van Ausdale, D. and Feagin, J.R. (2001) *The first R: How children learn race and racism*. Lanham, MD: Rowman & Littlefield.

FURTHER READING

Bowlby, J. (1979/2005) *The making and breaking of affectional bonds*. Abingdon: Routledge.

Gerhardt, S. (2004) *Why love matters: How affection shapes a baby's brain*. Abingdon: Routledge.

Jacobson, T. (2003) *Confronting our discomfort*: Portsmouth, NH: Heinemann.

Stern, D.N. (1990) *Diary of a baby*. New York: Basic Books.

Chapter 7

Play and its role in early learning

Nick Swarbrick

This chapter looks at the history of ideas about children's play.

OBJECTIVES

By the end of this chapter you will:
- be able to reflect on the work of major theorists;
- identify principles of play that derive from Vygotsky's work;
- make links between theories about play and practice.

Professional Standards for EYPS: S10, S11, S12, S13, S14, S16, S21, S26, S38, S39

Introduction

Psychologists and educators have found it difficult to come to a definition of what play is – partly, perhaps, because the phenomenon is more easily recognised than it is pinned down to a rigid classification. However, the complexities of play needs some unpicking. We can identify play when we see it, but going beyond a mere description is a more complex business. Vygotsky, for example, begins his discussion (1978, p92) of the role of play in development by describing what play is not, and Fisher is clear that 'there is no single definition of play, and, therefore, playful activities in one form or another have been open to interpretation in different ways.' (2002, pp 112–3).

The links with the next chapter – in which we will explore the notion of a curriculum – are to be found here in the idea that play is fundamental to what happens in the Early Years in all sorts of settings; play forms an integral part of the curriculum 'offer' in UK Early Years education and care.

Bruce's work has become, for many practitioners, the main way of looking at play. In the following extract, she revisits the themes explored in her classic work *Time to Play in Early Childhood Education* (Bruce, 1991). In this earlier work, Bruce describes play as having a number of dimensions, which receive different stress from different theorists. Play can be seen as recreation (pp36, 37); in this way of looking at it, play 'only takes place as a break from work', (1991, p57) so that playtime in a school reproduces the adults' desire to stop working with the children. Play can also be seen as preparation for adult life (p38), in which case play as genuinely child-centred is replaced by adult-led activities that children will find fun. In Bruce's theory, however, play is seen as an 'integrating mechanism' (1991, p55); a complex phenomenon in which the child brings together feelings, ideas and technical mastery. In the extract below, Bruce describes the essentials of this high-level play she calls 'free flow play'. It is worth noting that Bruce suggests that where seven or more of these features are present, 'we are likely to see effective learning.'

EXTRACT ONE

Bruce, T. (2004) Developing learning in early childhood. *London: Paul Chapman Publishing, pp148–150*

The essentials of play

Key themes

- *Research is showing how the brain uses first-hand experiences (feature no.1).*

- *Our understanding of rule-based behaviour in humans and other animals developing (feature no. 2).*

- *Play props (feature no 3) are being transformed by new technology (Newson and Newson, 1979: 235–8).*

- *We keep exploring the differences between the learning involved in choosing to play and adult-led learning (feature no. 4).*

- *Our understanding of pretending and role-play rehearsal for future life is increasing with work on symbol using (features nos. 5 and 6).*

- *The importance of personal space, as well as companionships and co-operative play, is another area of research which is continuing (features nos. 7 and 8).*

- *Our understanding of a child's developing possibility to have an interest and personal agenda is growing continually (feature no. 9).*

- *In this chapter we see young children wallowing and showing us their latest learning as they play (features nos. 10 and 11).*

- *This learning has a heart. Free-flow play has its own characteristics in action, making a co-ordinated whole (feature no. 12).*

The 12 features of free-flow play (Bruce, 1991, 1996, 2001a) emerged from the wealth of literature that exists on play either in English or translated into English. They have at times been called indicators for quality play (Bruce, 1996). They are a mechanism through which to think about play as it flows along. The observations can then be used to inform the planning, support the play and help children to extend their own play. The features apply to any age of child or adult (DFES, 2002), and can be used with children with special educational needs and disability throughout life. The 12 features of free-flow play draw on the areas of solidarity between theories and diverse disciplinaries, and converging evidence available about how to give holistic, consistent and coherent help to practitioners in developing play in ways which respect the depth of involvement children show at play.

When seven or more features are present during play, we are likely to see effective learning.

The 12 features of free-flow play (Adapted from Bruce, 1991)

1. In their play children use the first-hand experiences they have had in life.

2. Play does not conform to pressures to conform to external rules, outcomes, purposes or directions. Because of this, children keep control of their lives in their play.

3. Play is a process. It has no products. When the play ends, it vanishes as quickly as it arrived.

4 Children choose to play. It is intrinsically motivated. It arises when the conditions are conducive, spontaneously, and it is sustained as it flows.

5. Children rehearse the future in their play. Play helps children to learn to function, in advance of what they can do in the present.

6. Play takes children into a world of pretend. They imagine other worlds, creating stories of possible and impossible worlds beyond the here and now in the past, present and future, and it transforms them into different characters.

7. Play can be solitary, and this sort of play is often very deep. Children learn who they are and how to face and deal with their ideas, feelings, relationships and physical bodies.

8. Children and/or adults can play together, in parallel (companionship play), associatively or co-operatively in pairs or groups.

9. Play can be initiated by a child or an adult, but adults need to bear in mind that every player has his or her own personal play agenda (which he/she may be unaware of) and to respect this by not insisting that the adult agenda should dominate the play.

10. Children's free-flow play is characterized by deep concentration, and it is difficult to distract them from their learning. Children at play wallow in their learning.

11. In play children try out their recent learning, mastery, competence and skills and consolidate them. They use their technical prowess and confidently apply their learning.

12. Children at play co-ordinate their ideas and feelings and make sense of relationships with family, friends and culture. Play is an integrating mechanism which allows flexible, adaptive, imaginative, innovative behaviour. Play makes children into whole people, able to keep balancing their lives in a fast changing world.

97

EXTRACT ONE *continued*

1 First-hand experience used in play

Play feeds on real experience. It would be unethical to deprive children of normal experience on purpose, but there have been situations (such as in the Romanian orphanages) which demonstrate how lack of real experiences constrains the development of free-flow play with all its features.

A fundamental principle of early-childhood education is to give full opportunities to learn directly through the senses with freedom of movement, both indoors and outdoors. This opens up the potential for rich free-flow play, which depends also on rich experience if it is to bring depth to the development of learning. In high-quality play children in fact use many of the features of play.

Providing spaces and materials for play

In the St Francis Primary School nursery class, the staff make careful provision in the home corner, which is regularly reviewed and developed based on their observations, and is linked with curriculum areas of learning. At the period under discussion it was like this.

Bedroom area resources

Large bed for children/dolls

Small bed for children/dolls

Bunk beds for dolls

Unworkable TV with remote control

Chest-of-drawers for dolls' clothes

Mirror

Dressing-up clothes for children

Four dolls, two male, two female, multicultural

Accessories for babies: bottle, potty, toothbrush, small containers, etc.

It is worth noting how many practitioners use the term 'free-flow' to represent something different from the play Bruce is describing here. You can often hear practitioners describing the kind of Early Years set-up where children make their own choices about activities indoors and out as free-flow. The term accurately captures the image of a group of children moving easily through their environment. However, Bruce is not talking here about how children move or make choices about activities in their first educational surroundings, but uses a phrase from earlier theorists to suggest a play that is of a higher order than simple exploration.

Bruce's earlier work, *Time to play in early childhood education*, lays out the theory behind the extract we have been studying, and opens with a detailed overview of how play theory has developed since Friedrich Froebel in the nineteenth century. You may wish to refer, as a starting-point, to Chapters 2 and 3 of Bruce's *Time to play in early childhood education*.

POINTS TO CONSIDER

- *In what ways does Bruce's definition of play challenge you to rethink play?*

- *Do any of these 12 features seem more important to you than any others? If seven features might be seen as an indicator of effective learning, are some features essential components?*

- *Does Bruce's definition of free-flow play, in which she suggests that it can allow children to 'imagine other worlds, creating stories of possible and impossible worlds', hold true, or are children involved in play involved in what she describes as 'making sense of relationships with family, friends and culture'?*

- *The work of Laevers on how we can understand children's involvement in any activity, has been very important. His work in Belgium has influenced a number of research projects in the UK, notably the Effective Early Learning Project (Pascal and Bertram, 2001).*

- *You might want to spend some time observing a sustained session of play. How do you record play, so that the 'effective learning' can be seen by others? Is there a single method that will suit every situation?*

- *Watch an older child – perhaps of about five – deeply involved in an activity of their own choosing. Can you see evidence of any of the 12 features of free-flow play?*

In looking at features in play, we can often see repeating patterns, for example situations in which a child, alone or with others, explores different things using the same approach each time, or chooses to repeat activities. Nutbrown, using the Piagetian term 'schema', builds on the work of Athey (1990) to assert that these patterns of exploration and play are more than familiar approaches for a child; they illustrate 'forms of thought' and they can be used by practitioners to help them understand how a child learns best. The complexity of this theory can only be touched on here, but it is worth noting that, while the government's formal curriculum guidance has, until recently, avoided looking in detail at schema theory, there is increasing pressure on practitioners to understand how individuals learn and to cater for individual needs – see for example DfES (2006, p8). Might schemas be a way of describing how children learn through their play which practitioners can use to understand how best to cater for those children's needs?

EXTRACT TWO

Nutbrown, C. (1994) Threads of thinking. *London: Paul Chapman Publishing, pp10–11*

What are schemas?

We are now more knowledgeable about the learning patterns of babies and how they might think and learn. Goldschmied (1989) demonstrates how babies, given safe, stimulating and supportive opportunities, will use their senses to learn about objects they encounter. In so doing they enter into a world of discovery, puzzlement, social encounter and communication. Anyone who watches a young baby will see that some early patterns of behaviour (or schemas) are already evident. As babies suck and grasp, they rehearse the early schematic behaviours which foster their earliest learning. Early patterns of behaviour seen in babies become more complex and more numerous, eventually becoming grouped together so that babies and young children do not perform single isolated behaviours but coordinate their actions. Toddlers work hard, collecting a pile of objects in the lap of their carer, walking to and fro, backwards and forwards, bringing one object at a time. They are working on a pattern of behaviour which has a consistent thread running through it. Their patterns of action and behaviour at this point are related to the consistent back-and-forth movement. The early schemas of babies form the basis of the patterns of behaviour which children show between the ages of 2 and 5 years, and these in turn become established foundations for learning.

Athey (1990) maintains that children will notice elements from their surroundings, depending upon their interest at the time, and that they have their own intrinsic motivation which must be facilitated by materials and support from adults. She focused on how 2–5-year-old children also work on particular patterns of behaviour, referring to each of these patterns as a schema and defining a schema as: 'a pattern of repeatable behaviour into which experiences are assimilated and that are gradually coordinated' (ibid., p. 37). A number of patterns of behaviour were identified and named by Athey according to their characteristics. For example, the 'vertical schema' is so called because it relates to up-and-down movements. Athey discusses children's learning and development in terms of:

- *dynamic vertical;*

- *dynamic back and forth/side to side;*

- *dynamic circular;.*

- *going over and under;*

- *going round a boundary;*

- *enveloping and containing space;*

- *going through a boundary.*

The actions and marks related to these descriptions of movement can be identified in young children's drawing and mark-making, but Athey illustrates how such patterns can be represented in children's play, their thinking and their language. Athey argues that patterns pervade children's actions and speech as well as their mark-making. Detailed descriptions and discussion on ways in which different patterns of learning can be represented through action, speech and mark-making are given by Athey, who further illustrates in theoretical and practical terms how forms of thought (schemas), once identified, can be nourished with worthwhile content.

If a child is focusing on a particular schema related to roundness, we could say that the child is working on a circular schema. The form is 'roundness' and the content can be anything which extends this form: wheels, rotating machinery, rolling a ball, the spinning of the planets!

Similarly a child interested on 'up and downness' could be working on a vertical schema. The form is 'up and down'; related content can include using ladders, using the climbing frame, watching parascending or skydiving, riding in a lift or on an escalator. In the same way, if a child is interested in enclosing and enveloping schemas, the form is 'insideness', and related content may include wrapping presents, hatching chick eggs, en croûte cookery, mining and burrowing.

Why do some children seem obsessed with one particular activity, repeating it over and over again?

Liam was observed on many occasions putting cups, saucers, plates and other home-corner crockery in the home-corner sink. As soon as he had put all he could find into the sink he walked away and left them. This child might have been interested in spaces which contain and his own ability to put things inside things. He was perhaps seeking out experiences which enabled him to work on different aspects of enclosing and containing. Nursery staff needed to make further observations of Liam and, if the pattern was consistent, provide other ways of extending the 'enclosing' schema. Extension activities needed to embrace challenging curriculum content so that his thinking was extended. Children who are apparently repeating actions which seem aimless should be observed carefully by staff who can note precisely what children are doing. Staff can try to decide from their observations how valuable children's activities are. New experiences and interventions need to be based on detailed observations underpinned by the educator's knowledge of each child as an individual learner.

What happens to a schema once a child has established it?

Schemas, or repeatable patterns of behaviour, speech, representation and thought, can extend learning as they become fitted into children's patterns of thought. Early schemas seem to provide the basis for later learning. Athey (1990) describes how early 'back and forth' schemas can be observed in young children 'toddling and dumping'. Later 'back and forth' actions can be supported and extended with, for example, stories of 'going and coming' (see Chapter 7) or through experiences involving map-reading and map-making. Much more research is needed, but early schemas can connect together to provide the basis for later related experiences which can be assimilated into more complex concepts.

POINTS TO CONSIDER

- *Think about your chosen activities when you are not studying or working: do you have a preference for particular activities? Could any of these be grouped together in the way that Nutbrown describes?*

- *Think back to when you were a child: what were your activities like then? Why did you choose them?*

- *Look at the list of possible schemas. Can you identify any of them from your knowledge of children's play?*

- *If children have different preferences in how they choose or approach play activities as Nutbrown suggests, how does the practitioner organise a setting to encourage every child's learning?*

- *If you wish to read further about schemas, the work of Athey, on which Nutbrown bases her work, is seminal. Take some time to look at her major work,* Extending thought in young children *(Athey, 2006).*

Kitson puts forward a model of intervention in which the adult monitors, motivates and encourages. Duffy (2007, p4) discusses adults' intervening sensitively in children's play as 'often associated with periods of sustained shared thinking.' It is seen as critical to successful adult intervention that practitioners go beyond simplistic questioning that merely tests a child's understanding of adult concepts. 'Guess what's in my head', is a game practitioners play all too frequently, and the effective practitioner will try to look for a way to interact with children that sustains the play, motivates the wary and challenges children's thinking. The new curriculum documentation describes this kind of interaction: 'practitioners support and challenge children's thinking by getting involved in the thinking process with them', and suggests that:

> *Sustained shared thinking involves the adult being aware of the children's interests and understandings and the adult and children working together to develop an idea or skill.* (DfES 2007b: EYFS Card 4.3)

EXTRACT THREE

Kitson, N. (2005) Fantasy play and the case for adult intervention, in J. Moyles* The Excellence of Play, *2nd ed. Maidenhead: Open University Press, pp119–120

What do we mean by intervention?

Interventions allow for the development of structure within the children's socio-dramatic play. As with most forms of play, socio-dramatic play has a structure and rules but, as Garvey (1976) points out, these are often subsumed as part of the action. At first glance this structure is not apparent, but it is there nevertheless. Social play needs rules that we all understand in order for the interaction to take place. The adult becoming part of the play can facilitate the implementation of the rules as well as act as a behavioural model for the children to copy. Garvey (1976) further points out that in order to play we must understand what is not play. Part of this is helping the children differentiate between fantasy and reality. It is useful to identify clearly for the children when socio-dramatic play is taking place. This can be done very effectively by the adult working with the children saying, 'We are going to make up a story', or 'We are going to make up a play.' In this way the children are clear about the expectations of the activity and also have a much clearer idea of when they are, and are not, involved in the fantasy. It is equally important for the adult to make it really clear when the socio-dramatic play is over. This is merely the formalization of what children do for themselves. Their play will begin with, 'Let's pretend. . .' and will terminate when either the rules are broken or the children move away from the activity with, 'I'm not playing any more!' (Garvey 1976: 176).

Any episode of socio-dramatic play entails the exercises of shared imagination and the shared development of the theme of that particular episode. Young children are naturally egocentric and find it difficult to share. By selective interventions, able adults can monitor the negotiation of the children's ideas and act as facilitators. They can help the children remain consistent within their role and so aid the development of the story. One of the great strengths of this way of working is that through the fiction a great many learning areas can be explored. Problems can be set up which children can resolve within the story. The adult working within the fiction is able to set the problems and then keep the children on task, so making them confront the challenges. For example, in a children's story they have to get past the queen who guards the gate and into the castle. By having to persuade the queen to let them into the castle the children are employing and extending social skills. Their preferred solution may well have been to employ magic but such a solution would have merely avoided the social learning potential generated.

Intervention in socio-dramatic play enables the participating adult to keep the activity going by motivating the children to persist. While some children engage in such play readily, others need to be guided and encouraged to play a full part. The adult can help to refocus the story in order to bring the group together and generate excitement by introducing tension into the story. These are both essential to the development of socio-dramatic play but difficult for young children to attain for themselves. Working in a nursery school with a group of 18 children, I was asked to make up a drama on the theme of building. The children wanted to make up a story about building a house for the people in a book that had been read to them. After sorting out what had to be done, the work started. It was not long before the children began to lose concentration in the 'building' as there was little to hold their interest. In dramatic terms there was little or no tension. It was at this point that intervention was needed. I then pretended to receive a phone call from the boss who was going to come round and check up on our work. We would have to make sure that the house had been put together properly. Immediately the children were drawn back into the fantasy play and found a renewed vigour and purpose, created by the injection of tension and the pressure of evaluation. Equally effective could have been completing a given task in a set time (for example, 'We've got to build the hut before night comes'), meeting a challenge ('Do you think you could help me put out this fire?'), solving a problem ('What food should we give the animals now the snow's here?') or posing a dilemma for the children to work out ('But if we take the curing crystal how will the people who own it feel?'). These inputs into socio-dramatic play become the subtle tools of the adult working with children. Within the play, the adult is able to enrich and deepen the play and open up new learning areas for the children. S/he is able to intervene and structure the learning from within, without significantly reducing the children's ownership, a strategy Neelands (1984) defines as the 'subtle tongue' of the teacher.

It is important to remember that, although the adult can guide and to some extent shape the socio-dramatic play, essentially the play and action must be that of the children. Their ideas must be used. The words spoken must be their words expressing their thoughts. It may perhaps be that the adult simply joins in an existing 'game' with the children without the intention of simply being in the group but rather of moving the children's learning on, placing obstacles in the way of their story so that, by overcoming these obstacles, learning opportunities are created. A development of this is to construct the story with the children. 'What shall we make up a story about today?' Feeding from the children's ideas, both children and adult construct the fantasy. The adult's role is again that of facilitator, stretching and extending the children while maintaining interest and excitement. This adult participation legitimizes the play and encourages the children to see what they are doing as something valuable.

POINTS TO CONSIDER

- Kitson states that 'essentially the play and action must be that of the children'. Do you think his model of intervention risks taking the initiative away from the children?

- Kitson is talking in the first case about role play, where it might be seen as important to help children build a story with narrative 'tension', but does his model of intervention also apply to other areas of children's experiences, such as painting, or boisterous play outside?

- Have a look at May's book *Sound beginnings* (2006) to see how play can be organised with effective adult intervention.

Government guidance on 'target-setting' to improve children's experiences in the Foundation Stage is explicit in stating that a good target 'is as likely to be framed around child-initiated activity ("play") as around adult-led teaching' (DfES 2006, p5) and an OFSTED report (2007) criticised Early Years settings not only for insufficient attention to some of the aspects of communication, language and literacy but also for lower achievement in 'imaginative play because practitioners gave [it] too little attention' (p4).

You might find it of interest to look at the practice guidance that forms part of the Early Years Foundation Stage (DfES, 2007c). The reflective sections in the practice guidance (marked 'In depth') suggest that 'Listening to children enables practitioners to create meaningful activities that help them to make connections and tackle new ideas.' How does the practitioner do this? Is this something that the practitioner can plan for – or should it be spontaneous?

In some way, the lack of 'distance' between adult and child both engaged in problem-solving that has arisen during play is a mark of its naturalness; the adult isn't trying artificially to fulfil the role of the teacher, and the child may have abandoned the role of eager-to-please pupil. They are co-players, in much the same way as Anning and Edwards describe mother and child interactions (2006) – but they warn that this ease of interaction does not come effortlessly to the practitioner.

The 'In depth' section of the *Practice Guidance for the Early Years Foundation Stage* (DfES, 2007e) suggests that 'Through play in which they take the lead and make choices children develop their own thinking and encounter new ideas.' However, Kitson – and many of the other writers we explore in this book – see a role for the practitioner in extending and developing children's thought. There are implications here for the amount of time an adult can make available to work with a child or small group of children – and this, again, is where the notion of providing for play becomes closely related to issues of curriculum we see in the next chapter.

One way that practitioners might extend their repertoire of ways of interacting is to ask a colleague to look at these events in the course of a session. It would be possible for an adult, properly briefed, to observe their colleague with the specific intention of commenting on how the adult becomes involved in play, what kind of questions they use, and, perhaps most important of all, whether they are able to show a real sensitivity to the children's ideas and needs – and this ties in with Chapter 6, where we looked at the notion of the voice of the child, as well as to the notions of sustained shared thinking referred to elsewhere in this book.

It is clear from Vygotsky's classic work *Mind in society* (1978) that play allows a child to step into the zone of proximal development – which he described as 'the distance between the actual developmental level ... and the level of potential development ... under adult supervision or in collaboration with more capable peers' (1978, p86). Here Vygotsky describes it with the image, 'in play it is as though he were a head taller than himself'. However, there are some surprising assertions in the extract we are exploring; his view of play is that in its beginnings it is largely rehearsal, and in its later stages comprises rule-based games such as athletics or chess. He follows the argument of earlier writers in discussing competitive games and role play as if they were on a spectrum in which 'as play develops' it becomes more self-conscious and goal oriented. It is worth noting that his first examples here are drawn from socio-dramatic play, in which a child is remembering previous experiences and applying them imaginatively.

Vygotsky, L. (1976) Play and its role in the mental development of the child, in J. Bruner et al. (eds) Play: Its role in development and education. Harmondsworth: Penguin, p552

Is it possible to suppose that a child's behaviour is always guided by meaning, that a pre-schooler's behaviour is so arid that he never behaves with candour as he wants to simply because he thinks he should behave otherwise? This kind of subordination to rules is quite impossible in life, but in play it does become possible: thus, play also creates the zone of proximal development of the child. In play a child is always above his average age, above his daily behaviour; in play it is as though he were a head taller than himself. As in the focus of a magnifying glass, play contains all developmental tendencies in a condensed form; in play it is as though the child were trying to jump above the level of his normal behaviour.

The play-development relationship can be compared to the instruction-development relationship, but play provides a background for changes in needs and in conscious-ness of a much wider nature. Play is the source of development and creates the zone of proximal development. Action in the imaginative sphere, in an imaginary situa-tion, the creation of voluntary intentions and the formation of real-life plans and volitional motives – all appear in play and make it the highest level of pre-school development.

The child moves forward essentially through play activity. Only in this sense can play be termed a leading activity which determines the child's development.

The second question is: how does play move? It is a remarkable fact that the child starts with an imaginary situation when initially this imaginary situation is so very close to the real one. A reproduction of the real situation takes place. For example, a child playing with a doll repeats almost exactly what her mother does with her; the doctor looks at the child's throat, hurts him, and he cries, but as soon as the doctor has gone he immediately thrusts a spoon into the doll's mouth.

This means that in the original situation rules operate in a condensed and com-pressed form. There is very little of the imaginary in the situation. It is an imaginary situation, but it is only comprehensible in the light of a real situation that has just occurred; i.e., it is a recollection of something that has actually happened. Play is more nearly recollection than imagination – that is, it is more memory in action than a novel imaginary situation. As play develops, we see a movement towards the con-scious realization of its purpose.

It is incorrect to conceive of play as activity without purpose; play is purposeful activity for a child. In athletic games you can win or lose, in a race you can come first, second, or last. In short, the purpose decides the game.

> ### POINTS TO CONSIDER
>
> - This is a hard extract to read, especially since Vygotsky, a major
>   (here, at least) to be at odds with more recent writers' thinki
>   your initial response to try to agree with Vygotsky? Do you disag
>   he has to say – and if so, can you clarify why?
>
> - Is play the same for Bruce as it is for Vygotsky?
>
> - When looking at a group of children playing, what do you see? Highly devel-
>   oped play which involves the player 'wallowing in ideas' or children learning to
>   participate in competitive games or rehearsing the drama of their family lives?

According to Vygotsky the child is able, because he acts 'above his average age', to subor-dinate his desires to structures: to rehearsal and to goals. Without goals, play is, for Vygotsky, 'a dull game.' Vygotsky suggests that 'if there were no development in pre-school years of needs that cannot be realised immediately, there would be no play' (1976, p538). In the extract above Vygotsky is exploring further the idea of what play in early childhood might lead to, and sees that, in a typical developmental frame, children move towards playing games with rules, games that are competitive. When he says, controver-sially, that 'there is very little of the imaginary' in the situation he describes, you should note that he is seeing the play situation he is describing as a rehearsal of a previous experi-ence, and part of a spectrum that moves from simple exploration, through unfulfilled desire to wish-fulfilment and so on into complex competitive games with rules. It is worth remembering that the date of the original lecture delivered by Vygotsky is 1933; it may be that his perceptions of play, as his model of childhood, are affected by a feeling that child-hood as a period of considerable development and change needs to be defined by the 'end point' of that development, namely adulthood. Again, the introductory chapters of Bruce (1991), help set Vygotsky's thought in its historical context.

It is clear that Vygotsky sees play with an older or more capable child or an adult as essen-tial to assisting a child's development. He sees this development as needing a mentor: a play partner whose influence will allow the child to act 'a head taller than himself.' Bruce, on the other hand, sees free-flow play as possible for the child at play on his or her own. This difference can, perhaps, best be explained by Vygotsky's view that play leads some-where – while Bruce sees this high-level play as valid in itself, Vygotsky sees it as part of a developmental process.

You will have seen by now that play is a complex area of academic debate. Take some fur-ther time to observe play: in what ways can you see the play of a two-year-old as differing from that of a child at the end of the Foundation Stage?

If you can, watch the socio-dramatic play discussed by Vygotsky and Kitson. What is the role of the adult in any play you observe? If you are a co-player with children, in what ways do your interactions move the play forward? Do your actions and questions help children's thinking to develop? You might want to return to Chapter 3 to reflect further on children's learning.

...ct on the theories that practitioners draw on – often unconsciously – when they say ...at their approach is based on 'play-based learning'. Do they spend time involved in chil-...ren's play, or do they organise fun learning activities for the children in their care? Although *Time to play* (Bruce, 1991) remains a key text in play theory you may like to read in more detail some of the other theorists that underpin current practice.

We might choose to put the emphasis within play on aspects other than those Vygotsky describes, but nonetheless the notion that 'in play a child is always above his average age' is a powerful one. How do we organise experiences for children – at home, in a childcare or educational setting – which allows this flourishing, this 'highest level of pre-school development'?

Try to list the factors that might encourage play in any situation: are play partners important? What about time? Is the physical environment a central element for you? The Early Years Foundation Stage (DfES, 2007d) provides guidance for practitioners in these issues, especially in the 'Principles into practice' cards. You might try, with a colleague, to look at one of the four themes (DfES, 2007e, p5) and decide your own priorities in early childhood education and care.

Specifically you might consider Principles into practice Card 4.2 (DfES, 2007a), which discusses 'active learning'. Are you happy with this phrase as a 'shorthand' way of talking about children 'mentally or physically engaged in learning'? Or does it suggest to you that there is such a phenomenon as 'passive learning' in the Early Years? You might want to look again at Chapter 3 in the light of these government guidelines.

C H A P T E R   S U M M A R Y

Play is sometimes misunderstood, and in many ways the debate about what constitutes play is still unresolved. We will return in the next chapter to recent UK government statements on the place of play in the Early Years curriculum, but if you work with young children, or are thinking of doing so, you might reflect on the issues that this chapter raises. How do we define play in such a way that the adult's role is clear? Should we involve ourselves in children's play, and in what way?

REFERENCES

Anning, A. and Edwards, A. (2nd edn, 2006) *Promoting children's learning from birth to five*. Maidenhead: McGraw-Hill Education.

Athey, C. (2nd edn., 2006) *Extending thought in young children: a parent–teacher partnership*. London: Paul Chapman Publishing.

Bruce, T. (1991) *Time to play in early childhood education*. London: Hodder & Stoughton.

DfES (2006) Improving outcomes for children in the Foundation Stage in maintained schools **www.standards.dfes.gov.uk/primary/publications/foundation_stage/improving_outcomes/fs_imp_outcomes.pdf**.

DfES (2007a) Active Learning, Early Years Foundation Stage Card 4.2, **www.standards.dfes.gov.uk/eyfs/resources/downloads/card4_2.pdf** Accessed 27.03.07.

DfES (2007b) Creativity and Critical Thinking: Early Years Foundation Stage Card 4.3 **www.standards.dfes.gov.uk/eyfs/resources/downloads/card4_3.pdf** Accessed 27.03.07.

DfES (2007c) Effective practice: Supporting learning **www.standards.dfes.gov.uk/eyfs/resources/downloads/2_3_ep.pdf** Accessed 27.03.07.

DfES (2007d) Early Years Foundation Stage **www.standards.dfes.gov.uk/eyfs/site/index.htm** Accessed 27.03.07.

DfES (2007e) *Practice Guidance for the Early Years Foundation Stage* 00012-2007BKT-EN **www.standards.dfes.gov.uk/primary/publications/foundation_stage/eyfs/eyfs_guide12_07. pdf** Accessed 27.03.07.

Duffy, B. (2007) *All about ... messy play* Primary National Strategy 00012-2007BKT-EN, also available at **www.standards.dfes.gov.uk/eyfs/resources/downloads/4_3_c.pdf.**

OFSTED (2007) The Foundation Stage: A survey of 144 settings, HMI 2610.

Pascal, C. and Bertram, T. (2nd edn, 2001) *Effective Early Learning*. London: Paul Chapman Publishing.

Vygotsky, L. (1978) *Mind in society*. Cambridge, MA: Harvard University Press.

FURTHER READING

Fisher, J. (ed.) (2002) *The foundations of learning*. Buckingham: Open University Press.

Kalliala, M. (2005) *Play culture in a changing world*. Maidenhead: McGraw-Hill Education.

Laevers, F. (1993) Deep level learning: An exemplary application on the area of physical knowledge, *European Early Childhood Education Research Journal*, 1(1), 53–68.

May, P., Ashford, E. and Bottle, G. (2006) *Sound beginnings: Learning and development in the Early Years*. London: David Fulton.

Van der Veer, R. and Valsiner, J. (1991) *Understanding Vygotsky: a quest for synthesis*. Oxford: Blackwell.

WEBSITES

Planning for inclusion **www.qca.org.uk/10011.html.**

Kalliala's work is on **www.helsinki.fi/lehdet/uh/499f.html.**

The Effective Early Learning project is to be found at **www.worc.ac.uk/businessandresearch/ specialist/1230.html.**

More on the work of Ferre Laevers can be found at **www.cego.be/**

Chapter 8

Formal and informal curricula

Nick Swarbrick

OBJECTIVES

By the end of this chapter you should have:
- considered how a curriculum deals with complexities of relationships and communication as well as skills and knowledge transmitted;
- looked at the issues of how a curriculum is constructed;
- reflected on your role in organising the curriculum.

Professional Standards for EYPS: S1, S7, S8, S10, S11, S12, S13, S14, S39

Introduction

Why do we claim to base the curriculum of young children on play activities? Why do we have home corners? Why do we send children out to play for up to two hours a day on to freezing, barren school playgrounds? Why do we have reading schemes, unifix cubes, Lego or jigsaws? Why are we so nervous about 'teaching' creative activities or handwriting? Why do we have those mysteriously misnamed 'choosing times'? (Anning, 1997, pp9, 10)

When asked about why they chose to act in a certain way, a group of our students recently responded by saying things like 'I like the Reggio Emilia approach, so we do that when we can'; 'I picked up a lot from my training, but basically you do what works, don't you?' It seemed to suggest that, while practitioners make choices about their approach, some of their choices were down, not explicitly to principles, but to what seemed to work, based on every-day common sense. Some practitioners might even say that, while they would like to work a certain way, government intervention in terms of national strategies or a worry about being found wanting at inspection makes them work differently. There are certainly a number of pressures on Early Years practitioners about how they work with the children in their care.

When we look at what really happens in primary and Early Years education, a curriculum can appear, as Robin Alexander puts it (Alexander *et al.*, 1995), to be more of a jungle of historical roots, conflicting ideas and philosophies than it is a neat garden where everything is agreed and understood. When Early Years practitioners – and other educators – use the term 'curriculum', it is often supposed that the word means the content of the educational experiences offered, but, as this chapter explores, there is much more to it than this, and what we take for granted is, in fact, something to be thought through and negotiated, and something that has its roots in conventions of who children are and what they need.

What is clear is that Early Years practitioners need to think carefully about what they do and why they do it, so that they can plan to improve practice in their setting or defend existing practice. Who does the practitioner listen to? How does s/he make a case to a parent who is worried about a child's progress? How does s/he reflect the values the setting has developed in the work s/he does? Doing this kind of reflection links curriculum to the 'voice of the child' thinking already explored (see Chapter 6), and to reflecting on the role of play in Early Years, as we saw in Chapter 7 – and beyond the classroom to the complexities of decisions not only of teachers but also of locals and national policymakers (Aubrey, 2002).

In our first reading – which is a brief extract – we look at this place we think of as a learning institution, and see, supposedly through Paul's eyes, what being at school means to a small child. Liz Waterland's book is a fictionalised account of her research, intending to give a picture of 'the experiences the school offers its children, parents and staff' (1994, p7). You might want to ask yourself how valid her conclusions are, and whether this picture of being in the last weeks of the Reception class rings true for you.

EXTRACT ONE

Waterland, L. (1994) Not a perfect offering: A new school year. *Stroud: Thimble Press, pp30–31*

Paul had been sharpening his pencil, earnestly, into a rapier point which would snap again as soon as he tried to write with it. Both knew the time had come to stop. Paul blew the shavings out of the sharpener and put it back on the teacher's table. He looked critically at his pencil. That was the best point he'd managed all day. Save that one. He put the pencil carefully, and against rules, into his tray. Pencils were supposed to go into the pot for anyone to use but he had worked hard on that and no one else was going to have first go. Already he could anticipate the way he would touch the pencil on the paper to make a black, clear dot before, with a sudden jerk, the point would give and a tiny spray of lead would mar the sharpness of the dot. You drop dead with lead poisoning if it gets in your blood.

'Paul, sweep up the pencil sharpenings you've left, please.' His second favourite job. Smiling, Paul wrested the dustpan and brush away from Penny who was sweeping spilt sand.

'Mrs Cruickshank says I've got to have it now.' Penny gave up without a struggle and went to sit, rigidly upright, arms folded, chest nearly bursting as she thrust it upward to show how ready she was.

'Well done, Penny, you did get cleared up quickly!'

As for Sarah, she was delaying the process. Just another minute and the lace on the princess's dress would be finished. Kneeling on her chair, back turned towards the room, she coloured frantically, elbowing her protest as Robert tried to put the coloured pencils in the tub. It was no good, it was spoilt. Robert had jogged her arm and the colour had gone outside the lines. She surrendered the pencil to Robert, thumped him half-heartedly on the shoulder and took her book to Mrs Cruickshank. 'Look at my princess.'

'That's nice, Sarah. I like the lacy bit round her dress. Put it away now and come on the carpet.' Sarah looked at the picture as she walked to her tray. Mrs Cruickshank never noticed the bit outside the lines.

'Now, children. As you know, you're all getting too big to be in this class any more.'

'I'm five.'

'Yes, Tommy, I know, and so next year you'll be Year One children and be in a new class. Your teacher will be Mrs Dane.' At least that had finally been settled after all the staff discussions about who would have Year Two next year.

The children looked at each other in exaggerated delight and with noisy ooh-ing and ah-ing.

'I like her. She's all right.'

'I'm sure she'll be pleased to hear that, Paul, I'll tell her.' Occasionally, the temptation to a little irony, or even sarcasm, became too great. She really shouldn't do it, though, well aware that it was wasted on young children and resented by older ones.

POINTS TO CONSIDER

- If curriculum also implies a communication of values and expectations, how does this communication take place?

- How does Penny, for example, know the posture to sit in that gains the praise it does from Mrs Cruickshank, the teacher?

- What are your three most important beliefs about how children should be cared for or taught in Early Years education and care? You could look at the principles in the Curriculum Guidance for the Foundation Stage (QCA, 2000, p11) or think of your own.

- When you have read this extract, you might want to look at the first chapters of Kendall-Seatter's Reflective reader: Primary professional studies (2005) and Meighan and Siraj-Blatchford (1997), especially Chapter 6, 'The hidden curriculum: an overview.'

It would be easy to see Paul, Penny and the rest as representative of how childhood is for every child, or, perhaps more dangerously, of how it should be. Childhood can be seen, in many ways, as a social construct, a set of relationships and ideas that are brought together by members of society, rather than a universal truth. In this line of argument, we cannot talk about what a child should or shouldn't have as an experience, or what childhood looks like, as if it were the same experience for every child, but we take into account different perspectives from different sectors in society, and from an increasing awareness of how different childhood is in different cultures. The danger lies in the fact that, until practitioners and policymakers disentangle the issues of who it is we are dealing with, policy is likely to be formed without due consideration for the experience of Early Years education and day care from children's point of view, and practitioners are unlikely to be able to see clearly the possible gains and drawbacks of new initiatives or current practice.

Next time you visit a setting, observe a group of young children, and ask yourself:

- How do they know what to do?

- Ask two or more practitioners how they help children to settle in, and how they describe what goes on in their rooms to adults: Do they talk about learning? Enjoyment? Attitudes? Do they discuss the importance of play with parents, or do they highlight what children will learn?

What we believe about children affects how we relate to them. Brooker (2005) asks whether these constructs of childhood have remained constant over time. Her principal question here is to ask whether we have a sort of received wisdom that tells us 'what children are like'. The things we believe about childhood are crucial to what we do when we work with children: what we think children need; what we think children enjoy. In asking ourselves what we think children are like, we go back to Anning's set of questions above, and also to the issues that arose in previous chapters about what influences the family has, and what is the importance of play in a child's development. As the passage below from Brooker highlights, what we view as an 'ideal child' has implications for what we would view as the 'ideal environment'.

Before you read the extract below, note down as many brief descriptions of children as you can think of: 'little angels', 'little horrors', 'poor things', etc. What do any of these descriptions tell us about people's views of children? Are children essentially innocents, to be guarded from the influence of the world? Are they people who present with problems to be overcome? Needy figures to be rescued?

It is worth noting how Brooker talks about the 'ideological tradition' that gives rise to current practice in the UK. She is challenging the practitioner and the theorist to see the work done by childcare workers and educators as having roots in previous ideas and practice. Practitioners look, for example, at the principles of good Early Years practice (see, for example, QCA, 2000, pp11–13), but Brooker's argument is that we should see these as part of a long-standing practice that has grown up out of the work of thinkers and reformers such as Pestalozzi and the McMillans. This is not just a plea to take history seriously, however; here we are coming closer to the questions at the heart of this chapter about formal and informal curricula. We can make these decisions only when we understand something about the sort of people we are dealing with, and to do that we may need to unpick where our thinking comes from.

EXTRACT TWO

Brooker, L. (2005) **Learning to be a child: Cultural diversity and Early Years ideology,** *in N. Yelland (ed.) Critical issues in early childhood education. Maidenhead: Open University Press, p118*

Historians of childhood, whose work is increasingly widely read in the context of the new sociology of childhood (Mayall, 2002), have shown that constructions of childhood vary not only with the social and cultural setting in which they are situated, but also with the particular historical moments which shape those settings. In Britain, for instance, we know that medieval and Victorian childhoods were different from those of today; and that the childhood of poor children was never viewed in the same way as that of the rich (Hendrick, 1997). Other cultures have parallel histories. In every society, that is to say, the 'child' and 'childhood' are socially constructed concepts as well as lived realities – socially constructed by the powerful ideas and interests of the society, in response to its current economic and political needs, and religious and moral beliefs (James and Prout, 1997).

Institutions, however, create their own constructs, and it is widely recognized that the western, minority-world 'institution' of Early Childhood Education (Dahlberg et al., 1999) has evolved its own persistent, and passionate, view of childhood. The origin of these beliefs – in the philosophy of the Enlightenment and the project of modernity, and in the thinking of a pantheon of nineteenth- and twentieth-century 'pioneers' (Pestalozzi, Froebel, Owen, McMillan, Montessori, Isaacs) – is familiar, and frequently recounted (Anning,1991). The relationship of some aspects of this ideological tradition (Pollard et al., 1994) to the regimes of truth of develonmental psychology was proposed by Walkerdine (1984) and Burman (1994), and has been scrutinized more recently by those, like Dahlberg and her colleagues, who have been committed researchers in the early childhood field.

The concept of childhood contained in this ideological tradition or 'nursery inheritance' (Bennett et al., 1997) has undergone surprisingly little change over the past three centuries, a period in which national views of childhood have undergone frequent reversals (Hendrick, 1997): the natural and basically innocent child of Locke and Rousseau was present in Pestalozzi's school and Froebel's kindergarten, and subsequently in the nurseries of Owen and McMillan, Steiner and Isaacs. The concept had its heyday in the 1960s, when English nursery and infant schools were viewed internationally as a beacon of liberal and progressive practice. And it has held on, sustained by the idealism of practitioners and professionals, through periods of conservative backlash, to emerge in the 1980s and 1990s in the guise of Developmentally Appropriate Practice (Bredekamp and Copple, 1997). Ironically it is the latter manifestation which has triggered some of the sharpest critiques of the concept (see, for instance, Lubeck, 1996; Soto, 2002).

The ideology of Early Childhood Education, then, has constructed an enclosed and self-sufficient world within which such concepts are taken-for-granted, 'natural', 'self-evident' and 'true'. It is a tradition which both defines and defends its own realities, when necessary, creating barriers to protect itself and its children from harmful outside influences, usually those of governments intent on formalizing early learning.

EXTRACT TWO continued

An idealized picture of the 'Early Childhood' child might depict one who is:

- *full of potential, naturally curious, and eager to learn;*

- *active, outgoing and communicative;*

- *independent, autonomous, and able to show initiative;*

- *capable of selecting and sustaining self-chosen games and activities;*

- *able to learn through play and exploration.*

Such a child is assumed to develop through universal stages, common to all children.

The 'ideal environment' envisioned by the Early Childhood tradition for this 'ideal child' reflects these characteristics. It is a place which offers the time, space, opportunities and resources for active exploratory play, through which children can construct their own learning, at their own pace and in their own way. The 'play ethos' (as discussed by Smith, 1994, and Bennett et al., 1997) has therefore been seen as the key feature of such an environment.

POINTS TO CONSIDER

- *This, the longest extract in this chapter, explores the theory of an ideological tradition and then begins to explore how this is envisioned. People working with or studying young children know that each child will have some things in common with this idealised picture of the 'Early Childhood' child' and some things that don't sit quite so well with the image.*

- *Should we build our curriculum around what we 'know all children need'? Should we create record-keeping systems that detail children's individual needs to such an extent that it becomes impossible to get an overall view of the progress and attainment of any cohort in a school?*

- *What are the implications of either approach for supporting those times when a child moves further into the education system?*

Early Years workers can be confronted by a variety of voices urging more formal or more child-centred teaching and learning.

The argument for a formal approach might be summarised by thinking about children as 'eager to learn what we have to teach them' – in other words, since children can be seen, by and large, as happy to comply with adult requirements, we are in a good position to pass on the skills, knowledge and understanding that we judge they need, and that the best way to do this is with a clear lead from the adults and an amount of direct instruction. Along with this sometimes goes the argument that children need to have certain skills and knowledge early, so that they can make good progress later.

The argument for a less formal, more exploratory approach often draws on the 'nursery inheritance' that Brooker refers to. Children, it is argued, need time and space to develop at a crucial period in their lives, and we endanger their long-term development by misunderstanding or misinterpreting the requirements of an adult-dominated curriculum. First-hand experience and time to play in ways that children choose with materials such as sand, block play are the best foundation for later learning.

The people who plan for the activities a child may undertake in a session are responsible for the quality of those experiences. They should be able to defend the experiences they plan in terms of their understanding of 'good practice', and in terms of what they know about a child's development. The current *Curriculum Guidance for the Foundation Stage* (QCA, 2000) asks practitioners to give consideration to a pedagogy in which play is a major way in which learning takes place. A wide number of books advocate child-initiated activity and the research cited at the end of this chapter sees a balance between what children explore in their own ways and on their own terms and what adults decide to do with children as a measure of how healthy the learning environment is.

Many practitioners would describe their work as 'child-centred,' or 'play-based,' and the latest documents on the Early Years Foundation Stage in England talk explicitly about play, while still requiring specific input into children's learning experiences in order to 'improve outcomes'. (DfES, 2006). The following extract challenges us to examine what this means in practice.

EXTRACT THREE

DfES (2007) The Early Years Foundation Stage Practice Guidance. *00012-2007BKT-EN, pp6–7*

Play (Principles into Practice cards)

1.16 Play underpins the delivery of all the EYFS. Children must have opportunities to play indoors and outdoors. All early years providers must have access to an outdoor play area which can benefit the children. If a setting does not have direct access to an outdoor play area then they must make arrangements for daily opportunities for outdoor play in an appropriate nearby location. The EYFS CD-ROM also contains information suggesting innovative ways to engage children in outdoor play.

1.17 Play underpins all development and learning for young children. Most children play spontaneously, although some may need adult support, and it is through play that they develop intellectually, creatively, physically, socially and emotionally.

1.18 Providing well-planned experiences based on children's spontaneous play, both indoors and outdoors, is an important way in which practitioners support young children to learn with enjoyment and challenge. In playing, children behave in different ways: sometimes their play will be responsive or boisterous, sometimes they may describe and discuss what they are doing, sometimes they will be quiet and reflective as they play.

EXTRACT THREE *continued*

1.19 The role of the practitioner is crucial in:

- *observing and reflecting on children's spontaneous play;*

- *building on this by planning and resourcing a challenging environment which:*

    - *supports and extends specific areas of children's learning;*

    - *extends and develops children's language and communication in their play.*

1.20 Through play, in a secure but challenging environment with effective adult support, children can:

- *explore, develop and represent learning experiences that help them to make sense of the world;*

- *practise and build up ideas, concepts and skills;*

- *learn how to understand the need for rules;*

- *take risks and make mistakes;*

- *think creatively and imaginatively;*

- *communicate with others as they investigate or solve problems.*

POINTS TO CONSIDER

- *This extract seems to give the practitioner the directive that play should 'underpin the delivery', of the curriculum but in what way does it inform the practitioner about what play should look like?*

- *Should children take the lead in exploring their environment?*

- *If a practitioner were to base her/his practice with regard to play on this, what might they tell parents?*

- *Look at an Early Years equipment catalogue, and find a section dealing with large play equipment such as climbing frames or vehicles. Try to determine who decided to have those things available in the setting. Where does the notion of 'standard' equipment come from?*

- *List five things in an average Early Years setting that would be generally available to a young child without adult guidance. Note down: How would the child explore them? Would adult assistance improve the experience?*

The Early Years Foundation Stage gives practitioners explicit permission to organise Early Years education around play – and yet there remains a tension between a play-based curriculum and one in which the adults know and plan for particular end-points or outcomes. Can we resolve this tension? We have to debate whether 'child-centredness and curriculum-centredness are a simple either/or' (Edwards and Knight, 1994, pp32, 33). Looking at these recent statements on the value of play allows us to reflect on what we value most in the Early Childhood curriculum. Jarvis's insight is very interesting here: 'There has almost been a belief that once we know the aims and objectives of the lesson and the content to be taught, then the method is self-evident.' (2006, p30). Yet we can see that, in Early Years especially, this is not the case.

It is very easy to fall into thinking that child-centred or curriculum-centred curriculum development is, of itself, flawed, and leads to excesses. The caricature description of one would be that adults either fail to participate and simply observe, and the other, adults dominate children's activity to such as degree that child-initiated activity is seen as worthless. Some of the debates around the formal curriculum and young children stem from this kind of misrepresentation of the 'other' argument. However, a lot of good Early Years practice has a sensitive mix of both adult-led and child-initiated activity. Children engaged in their own activities are not left to themselves by the adults, but are observed and their experiences are thought through after the session, and used as a basis for further exploration and play the next day. Similarly, in good provision, adult-led activity is developed sensitively from children's interests and from what the adults have observed a child can 'nearly do' – the Vygotskian zone of proximal development we met earlier. It is this idea that leads the extract we have explored to frame the role of the practitioner as 'crucial' in 'observing and reflecting', 'planning and resourcing'.

We have already (Chapter 7) met the idea that adults becoming involved in children's play helps children 'get the most out of' the play they are engaged with. This next passage from Bilton's work suggests a number of practical approaches to adapting current provision in order to maximise the potential for individual children or groups. Her book goes on to explore the role of the adult, but you can see in this extract how the adult might be seen as a guide to the potential of a certain piece of equipment or a way of playing.

EXTRACT FOUR

Bilton, H. (2002) **Outdoor play in the Early Years.** *London: David Fulton, pp77–78*

Taking the curriculum to the children

As it appears that boys are not achieving as well as they should at school, it would seem that schools should be more 'boy friendly'. They need to consider doing it 'both gender ways' and may need to let Jack 'climb the beanstalk first'. It would appear that failure at school starts early and that help and intervention need to start as soon as possible. Boys are very movement-orientated – they like to build and construct and they enjoy acting out and playing imaginative games with others. It would seem then that schools need to consider how to 'take the curriculum' to these children, as opposed to expecting them to access the curriculum as they are clearly not succeeding in this at present. It would seem that outdoors is a preferred place for boys and perhaps if the curriculum is taken to boys in this environment they may be able to access it more easily. This means that not only must Foundation Stage staff make outdoor play interesting, but they also must get more involved in the play and devise ways to fit the more formal components of the curriculum into this setting.

As educators we have a brief to ensure that everyone has equality of access to the whole curriculum. Girls are clearly not getting this equality; some activities are being denied them because of domination by boys, some activities are being denied because as a group, girls tend to want adult presence.

Margaret McMillan considered that all children would benefit from nursery education but that they would all get different things from it. For example, the children from the affluent parts of Chelsea were nicknamed the Kensington Cripples by the middle class parents who set up the Open Air Nursery in the 1930s, because they had every-thing done for them by servants and could do little for themselves (Whitbread 1972, p. 72). McMillan felt this group could benefit from simply doing things for them-selves.

'Taking the curriculum to children' can simply mean having an adult present who participates in play, protecting children from others who may want to take over, and showing the potential of the material to those involved. But it also means giving the children confidence to use the materials. How adults can support children is dis-cussed in greater detail in the next chapter.

Taking the curriculum to the children may simply mean moving activities, such as lan-guage and mathematical games, books and tapes, from indoors to outdoors. The presence of such activities outdoors, in what some children may feel is a less pres-surised and freer atmosphere, may be the spark to enable children to use the materials. One particular child I remember in a nursery was very reticent about paint-ing, gluing, digging and using sand and water. He was a child who enjoyed outdoor play and physical activity. Staff had tried various approaches to help him use these materials and then one day foot-printing was offered outside. He very eagerly took his socks and shoes off and got 'stuck into' the foot-printing. One cannot say that this experience caused him to start using paint, to dig or work in the sand but, coin-cidentally, it was after this experience that he started joining in with those activities.

Likewise, a teacher in a nursery class was concerned that a number of the girls seemed to be monopolising the home corner and a number of boys were controlling the block area. One evening she simply swapped the position of these two learning areas and the next day the boys went to the same place as before but discovered the home corner and the girls went to the same area and found the blocks. What was even more surprising was the way in which both groups took up roles appropri-ate to that area, with the boys playing a home scene and the girls constructing with the blocks.

Taking the curriculum to the children may involve wrapping it up in the play the chil-dren are involved in, so that what they might consider 'work' indoors they will consider as play outdoors. Imaginative play indoors often involves reading and writ-ing through, for example, note-taking in the doctor's surgery, adding up a bill in a shop, reading the newspaper at home. In schools involved in good outdoor play these activities are naturally added to imaginative play outdoors. And so children have notepads to take orders at a café, children write down the weather forecast for the farmer, children make maps of where the treasure is buried in a pirate scene. Children have opportunities to make number tags, labels for different events, score-cards for an imaginative sports scene. Staff organise number games in the gymnasium area where children have to stand at a particular number if wearing a particular colour, or games where children have to read what the card tells them to do – '4 skips' or '6 jumps', but alongside will be a drawing to help explain the words. Staff use chalk on the ground for all sorts of number and letter recognition games. They even use the playground surface as a piece of paper and have a game of rhyming where they use the surface of the playground to write down the words.

Simply bringing aspects of the more formal curriculum outdoors may encourage some children to use that knowledge indoors, and make signs, notices, lists and the like, at the graphics table. As Paley (1984) found when she extended the play period, boys used the extra time to get involved in more work-orientated activities and the girls engaged in more imaginative play.

In conclusion

All children have a right to access all activities and experiences in school. It would make sense that they do this in the easiest possible way. In this chapter it has been suggested that some children may prefer to play outdoors and that some children's play and behaviour may be different when outdoors compared to when indoors – they become more interested, more assertive, less inhibited or can concentrate more easily. This is so for both boys and girls but seems particularly pertinent to boys, who tend to want to play outdoors and who are more physically active, more keen to learn through exploration and interested in exploring superhero roles. It has also been suggested that some girls are not able to play as they would like or have the potential to do so outside, as boys tend to dominate many of the movable and con-structive activities and staff are not present to support their endeavours.

In 1972 Hutt argued that boys and girls were different and needed to be treated as such: this would seem to be a message which needs revisiting. Girls seem more ready to fit the school system and as a consequence do well; on the other hand, many boys find school difficult and as a consequence are underachieving. To help all children reach their full potential it would seem beneficial to make the school system fit the needs of the children rather than expecting children to fit the school system. By offer-ing the curriculum in an environment which children feel comfortable in and in a way they have knowledge of, may help boys to be more successful in learning. To enable girls to access the rich resources outdoors may involve staff supporting these children in their play and being with them to give them confidence. For this to happen staff need to make the outdoor play interesting, take the whole curriculum outdoors, and work and play alongside children in the outdoor setting. In this way all children, girls and boys, may have equality of access to the curriculum.

POINTS TO CONSIDER

There are some big questions to be thought through here.

- *How does the practitioner know when to intervene?*

- *Is it about policing behaviour, or instruction?*

- *Is play a private world for children?*

- *Can this level of interaction be sustained where the curriculum is led in such a way that the adults' time is taken up in direct teaching?*

There is another side to this, however. Bilton's book concentrates on the outdoor experiences of young children. Before moving on, reflect:

- *Do you enjoy being out of doors when not working/studying?*

- *What do you do?*

- *Do you think there are advantages to providing outdoor play experiences for children?*

- *What might the drawbacks be?*

When you have read this extract, you could follow up the notion of effective intervention in children's play by looking at Siraj-Blatchford's report (a project related to the EPPE research, see below) on effective pedagogy:

www.dfes.gov.uk/research/data/uploadfiles/RR356.pdf

Section 4.2 (pp43 ff) has some very good examples of episodes of effective thinking with children.

It is clear from the major research reports of EPPE and SPEEL (there are links at the end of this chapter) that sensitive intervention from adults can make all the difference between a good learning experience and an excellent one. Adults supporting children's learning can be on hand to ask questions that will move a child's thinking along, or they may be able to give some direct instruction that will help a child in another situation. But when to intervene? We come to understand how children learn by observing and reflecting on their learning. When you know what this child or that child is interested in, what they can and can't do – and, most important of all, what they can nearly do – then knowing whether now is the right moment to join in is a simpler task. The experienced practitioner doesn't always get this right: we might expect children to be able to do this, or that, but one of the things that makes watching and working with children so interesting for the adult is that we can always be surprised.

As for being outside with children, it is worth noting that Bilton recognises that this can be problematic for some Early Years workers, especially if they are used to thinking of inside as a place where they feel comfortable in their practice. One way of looking at this is to think in terms of children's entitlement: are we going to restrict children by not supporting their learning and development in all areas of their lives? What messages do we pass on to children by appearing to be inactive, unwilling to explore or take risks?

What are the implications for staffing that this model of teaching and learning requires? Should we have better child–adult ratios, or is this more an issue of training and management?

Look at a setting you know or work in: what are the adult–child ratios? Do these allow staff sufficient time to engage in purposeful discussions with children?

Spend some time in the setting observing an adult. Note the number of times they intervene in a child's learning. Reflect on (or ask them) what they may have hoped would be the outcome of the discussion they had with the child.

Returning to the theme of quality, take a look at two major studies that inform the government's present thinking about Early Years pedagogy: the SPEEL project and the EPPE project:

www.dfes.gov.uk/research/data/uploadfiles/RB363.pdf

www.ioe.ac.uk/schools/ecpe/eppe/index.htm

The conclusions they come to are remarkably similar: effective Early Years practice requires a balance of activities that are initiated by adults and ones children have chosen themselves; this requires adults working with children to be sensitive to the developmental needs of the children, and to be able to become involved in a responsive and thoughtful way.

In the light of these research reports, it is interesting to look at what good and not-so-good quality teaching and learning look like from OFSTED's point of view:

www.ofsted.gov.uk/assets/3655.pdf

This report urges settings to set 'appropriate challenges', and notes that, too often, children sit for long periods even in the early days of school; that activities are not always matched well to pupils' differing needs.

Given the extract from Bilton above, it is worth noting that the report praises, 'the provision of first-hand experiences, *both indoors and outdoors*'.

C H A P T E R   S U M M A R Y

We have looked at some of the major components of the Early Years curriculum. This chapter recognises how there is still some debate about how much adults control children's learning. It asks the reader to think about the influences on how children learn from the point of view of a young child, and to reflect on the role of the adult in organising experiences for children. Central to this is the notion that we need to try to figure out what each of us understands by the question 'What is a child?' since the way we work with young children will, to some degree, depend on our answer to this crucial question.

REFERENCES

Alexander, R., Willcocks, J., Kinder, K. and Nelson, N. (1995) *Versions of primary education*. Abingdon: Routledge.

Anning, A. (2nd edn, 1997) *The first years at school*. Buckingham: Open University Press.

Aubrey, C. (2002) Multiple perspectives on growing up in an urban environment, *European Early Childhood Education Research Journal*, 10(2), 63–84.

Bilton, H. (2002) *Outdoor play in the Early Years*. London: David Fulton

Brooker, L. (2005) Learning to be a child: Cultural diversity and Early Years ideology, in N. Yelland (ed.) *Critical issues in early childhood education*. Maidenhead: McGraw-Hill Education.

DfES (2006) *Improving outcomes for children in the Foundation Stage in maintained schools*. Ref: 03960-2006BKT-EN.

DfES (2007) *The Early Years Foundation Stage Practice Guidance* 00012-2007BKT–EN.

Edgington, M. (2004, 3rd edn) *The foundation stage teacher in action: teaching 3, 4 and 5 year olds*. London: Paul Chapman Publishing.

DfES Curriculum Guidance for the Foundation Stage (QCA, 2000).

Edwards, A. and Knight, P. (1994) *Effective early years education: Teaching young children*. Buckingham: Open University Press.

Fisher J. (2002, 2nd edn) *Starting from the child*. Buckingham: Open University Press.

Jarvis, P. (ed.) (2nd edn, 2006) *The theory and practice of teaching*. Abingdon: Routledge.

Kendall-Seatter, S. (2005) *Reflective reader: Primary professional studies*. Exeter: Learning Matters.

Meighan, R. and Siraj-Blatchford, I. (3rd edn, 1997) *A sociology of educating*. London: Cassell.

Siraj-Blatchford, I., Sylva, K., Muttock, S., Gilden, R. and Bell, D. (2002) *Researching effective pedagogy in the early years*. Research Report No 356, DfES.

QCA (2000) *Curriculum Guidance for the Foundation Stage*. London: QCA.

Waterland, L. (1994) *Not a perfect offering: A new school year*. Stroud: Thimble Press.

WEBSITES

www.dfes.gov.uk/research/data/uploadfiles/RB363.pdf

www.ioe.ac.uk/schools/ecpe/eppe/index.htm

www.ofsted.gov.uk/assets/3655.pdf

www.froebelweb.org/gifts

www.communityplaythings.com/c/Resources/Articles/BlockEssay.htm

Chapter 9
Professionalism in the Early Years

Rachel Friedman

O B J E C T I V E S

By the end of this chapter you should have:
- further considered *why* reflecting on issues around professionalism is critical to Early Years practitioners;
- critically evaluated *what* changes are currently taking place in the field of early childhood education;
- analysed *how* the changes have implications for your work with young children and their families.

Professional Standards for EYPS: S24, S33, S34, S35, S37, S38, S39

As you work through this chapter you will find it useful to be aware of the changes that are being made in the Early Years (**www.cwdcouncil.org.uk/projects/earlyyears.htm**; **www.standards.dfes.gov.uk/eyfs/; www.surestart.gov.uk**). As this book goes to press, changes include the introduction of the Early Years Foundation Stage, continued development of Early Years Professional Status, growth in the number of Children's Centres, and more intentional multiprofessional work focused around the child that reflect the changing nature of the field. These changes impact on families of young children, young children, those working in the field and students, at all levels, studying the care and education of young children. You might find it helpful to share your findings with your colleagues and discuss how and whether these changes contribute to professionalism in the field.

Introduction

We will start this chapter by looking at the experience of one early childhood practitioner. This is done with the intention that it will motivate you to reflect on your own story of working with young children and the issues of professionalism that this work raises for you. Professionalism is a challenge that those working in the field of early childhood face at all career stages.

Jenny is an early childhood practitioner. She has recently earned a BA in early childhood studies. Jenny believed that she officially started her career as an early childhood practitioner once she earned her degree. Prior to earning her degree she had been employed by early childhood settings as an associate practitioner working with children from birth through five in various settings. As a new Early Years practitioner in the 1990s Jenny was free to create her own plans, working with other staff in the setting. She found that in both the private and public-sector settings there was limited central guidance or expectations about curriculum, planning or assessment, although the emphasis was explicitly on child-centredness. It appeared that parents were concerned about their child's ability to separate from them with ease, make friends, be stimulated and bring home pieces of work to be displayed. In her first experiences there was limited demand for curriculum plans. Jenny liked being able to look through her records and seeing what she planned and how the children had progressed. The other kind of record-keeping that she adopted, she had learned as an early childhood student, and that was to keep an observation journal. In this journal she would note observations and conversations in order to keep records of children's experiences and to develop a greater understanding of the 2-, 3-, 4- and 5-year-olds in her care.

In the first setting in which she worked Jenny had two colleagues who were at polar ends of the planning spectrum. One colleague was a former Reception teacher and the other was pursuing an advanced certificate in Early Years education. Jenny knew these women both as colleagues and as the teachers of her two children.

The former Reception teacher taught the children that were in their last year prior to starting statutory education. Her room was organised with many different learning 'centres'. She posted her weekly plans for all to see. Most of the materials in her classroom were purpose-designed for early childhood settings. Her display boards were organised and balanced with borders that were not only laminated but also matched the topic of study. She sent home weekly newsletters detailing the learning in her room.

The other colleague worked very differently. Her plans were inspired by events that happened to her on her way home or on the way to work. She was also flexible with her plans and easily 'integrated the children' in the curriculum. When one of the children came to school with stitches in the palm of her hand, all of the children spent the day exploring water play, playdough and other 'messy activities' wearing rubber gloves. The display boards displayed the children's work but also items that were not created intentionally for children (e.g. posters of different countries donated by a travel agency). Parents learned about the curriculum on a daily basis; at the end of each session the teacher and children would prepare a poster-size memo summarising of the events of the day.

Working alongside these two colleagues was an enlightening experience and was the catalyst for intense self-reflection. Jenny questioned the view of herself as a professional teaching in an early childhood setting and the view of many others that early childhood teaching was not a professional occupation. What did it mean? What did it look like? Were her colleagues 'teaching'? Was she 'teaching'? Did we need to keep records of young children? Who would read them? Why would anyone read them when Jenny and her colleagues were perceived by others to be baby-sitters?

As an early childhood teacher Jenny and her colleagues relied heavily on the work of Piaget and Bruner. Building on the work of Mcmillan, Issacs and Froebel, voices such as those of Curtis, Bruce, David and Lally were growing stronger during those years. Ideas of diversity (ILEA, 1983), taking on the ideas of the children, listening to young children (Paley, 1986), project approach (Katz and Chard, 1989), and acknowledged that parents are the first teachers of young children. They read stories, sang songs, explored with art and science and explored kinaesthetically, went on trips in the community and spent time out of doors. In addition Jenny and her colleagues were encouraged to take up opportunities for in-service training. Jenny and many of her colleagues were active members in the local branches of the British Association for Early Childhood Education (BAECE). They took pride in their work and the accomplishments of the children.

In spite of all of that Jenny and her colleagues were bringing to their work, the overall satisfaction that parents had, the changes that were noticed in the children throughout the year and in the children as they moved from one year group to another, the nagging questions remained. Jenny wondered whether she was a professional. Were her colleagues professionals? And if so, what made them professional? I hope that you will consider asking these questions of yourselves.

Untangling professionalism in the Early Years

Professionalism in the Early Years is like a ball of knotted string. In order to untangle the string, all of the other knots must be opened. The knots of professionalism in Early Years include issues around gender, the socialisation of women, the power status of the clients, definitions of profession, ethics, women's roles in society, compensation, leadership, change that comes from outside of the field, Early Years Professional Status and the other multitude of changes that come from policy initiatives which have been referred to in several chapters of this book.

You might find it helpful to look at some of the early childhood writers who continue to work at loosening the knots:

- Moyles (2001) explores the paradox of the passion that many early childhood practitioners refer to in their work which might yet be what prevents us from being perceived as professionals.

- Osgood (2006) explores the link between 'notions of "professionalism" and gendered identity construction against the backdrop of increased state regulation and demands for performativity in the Early Years' (p187).

- Rodd (2006), in her third edition of *Leadership in early childhood*, has dropped the subtitle 'the pathway to professionalism' yet she continues to link leadership with professionalism.

- Siraj-Blatchford *et al.* (2007), in their discussion of the 'Team around the child', explore the nature of multiprofessional team working.

Challenges of definitions

The topic of professionalism is inherently complex, but the discourse of professionalism within early childhood is even more complicated. This does not mean that we need to abandon the discussion; rather I would argue that we need to work together to strengthen our footing and position. We need to reach out to all of those working with young children and encourage dialogue. This can be achieved by working through early childhood organisations and demanding that professionalism be put on the agenda. If we do not care for ourselves, our interests will not be made a priority.

'What it means to be professional, to show professionalism or to pursue professionalization is not universally agreed or understood' (Hargreaves and Goodson, 1996, p4). Early childhood practitioners and teachers, nursery nurses and family-care providers are not alone in the struggle to come to grips with the terminology. However, this does not excuse us from not taking responsibility for our livelihood.

Those defining 'professional' have not typically shed a favourable light on women and the professions to which women gravitate (Etzioni, 1964; Howe, 1980 in Fromberg, 1997). Is this because this discourse has been heavily influenced by men or because it is an accurate appraisal of the little autonomy that we have or because we do not have authentic professional status? Or is it because women who are in the majority in our field are not comfortable with taking on leadership roles?

POINTS TO CONSIDER

- *What motivated you to work with young children?*

- *Do you see yourself as a professional in your setting?*

- *What skills do you need to learn or adopt in order to be a professional and to be perceived by others as a professional?*

- *How can you contribute to the professionalism of the field?*

Professionals in a profession?

Definitions of 'profession' include aspects of training, specialised knowledge, ethical practice, autonomy, control of entry into field, professional bodies (Fromberg, 1997). These aspects of 'profession' appear to be a definition that we ought to be able to work with in the field of early childhood.

Let us examine more closely some of the components of the definition.

- **Specialised training**. There are opportunities for education for those at all levels of the field. There are A-level courses available in further education (FE) colleges, Foundation degrees, BAs, MAs, and doctorates. In addition there exist a multitude of continuing education opportunities available from a wide range of sources.

- **Specialised body of knowledge**. Is the body of knowledge we possess critical? Increasingly this has become the case. With more parents in the workforce, more children are in need of early care and education. This specialised body of knowledge must include child development, communication skills, knowledge about the impact of issues of inclusion (SEN, EAL, culture, ethnicity, gender, sex, ability, etc.).

- **Professional organisations**. We have access to both local professional organisations (e.g. British Association of Early Childhood Education (BAECE), National Childminding Association of England and Wales (NCMA), NIPPA – the early years organisation) and international organisations with local branches such as l'Organisation Mondiale pour l'Education Préscolaire (OMEP UK National Committee).

- **Autonomy**. The issue of autonomy in the field of Early Years is an issue that needs to be addressed at all levels. Seeing this in print makes it appear 'easy'; however, the reality is harsh and is experienced on all different levels of the field. What exactly does this mean? To what extent do experienced, qualified and capable practitioners feel constrained by rather than supported by national policy drivers?

POINTS TO CONSIDER

- *Using the broad definition of profession, consider whether you are a member of a profession.*

- *Can a person be professional if they do not work in a recognised profession?*

- *What are the changes that need to take place in order for those working in the Early Years to be recognised as members of a profession?*

- *What changes could you make to become a professional in a profession?*

- *With what professional organisation are you affiliated?*

CHAPTER SUMMARY

There are many challenges in the field of early childhood at present. These could, however, be presented, and experienced, as opportunities rather than challenges.

The growth and proliferation of Early Childhood Studies courses, and the introduction of the new Early Years Professional Status, are both indicators of the way in which the area is seen as a national priority.

What does seem certain is that the momentum of change looks set to continue for some time yet. We hope that through engaging with the readings and questions contained in this book, you will feel more ready for the challenges and opportunities as they present themselves.

REFERENCES

Bruner, J. (1986) *Actual minds, possible worlds*. London: Harvard University Press.

Bruce, T. (1987) *Early childhood education*. London: Hodder and & Stoughton.

Curtis, A. (1986) *A curriculum for the pre-school child: Learning to learn*. Windsor: NFER-Nelson.

Early Years Curriculum Group (1988) *Early childhood education: The early curriculum and the national curriculum*. Stoke on Trent: Trentham Books.

David, T. (1991) *Under five-under educated?* Milton Keynes: Open University Press.

Etzioni, A. (1964) *Modern organisations*. Englewood Cliffs, NJ: Prentice-Hall.

Fromberg, D. (1997) The professional status of early childhood educators, in J. Isenberg, and M.R.C. Jalongo, (eds.) The professional and social status of the early childhood educator: Challenges, Controversies and Insights. NY: Columbia Teachers College Press.

Hargreaves, A. and Goodson, I. (1996) Teachers' professional lives: Aspirations and actualities, in I. F. Goodson and A. Hargreaves (eds) *Teachers' professional lives*. Abingdon: Falmer Press, pp1–27.

Inner London Education Authority (ILEA) (1985) *Race, sex and class*. London: Inner London Education Authority.

Katz, L.G. and Chard, S.C. (1989) *Engaging children's minds: The project approach*. New Jersey, NJ: Ablex.

Lally, M. (1991) *The nursery teacher in action*. London: Paul Chapman Publishing.

Moyles, J. (2001) Passion, paradox and professionalism in Early Years education, *Early years*, 21(2), 81–95.

Osgood, J. (2006) Professionalism and performativity: the feminist challenge facing Early Years practitioners. *Early Years*, 26(2), 187–199.

Paley, V.G. (1986) *Mollie is three: Growing up in preschool*. Chicago, IL: University of Chicago Press.

Rodd, J. (2006) *Leadership in early childhood* (3rd edn). Maidenhead: McGraw-Hill Education.

Siraj-Blatchford, I., Clarke, K. and Needham, M. (2007) *The team around the child*. Stoke on Trent: Trentham Books.

Index